Management Extra

INFORMATION AND KNOWLEDGE MANAGEMENT

Management Extra

INFORMATION AND KNOWLEDGE MANAGEMENT

ELSEVIER

eLEARN

Pergamon
Flexible
Learning

AMSTERDAM • BOSTON • HEIDELBERG • LONDON • NEW YORK • OXFORD • PARIS •
SAN DIEGO • SAN FRANCISCO • SINGAPORE • SYDNEY • TOKYO

Pergamon Flexible Learning is an imprint of Elsevier
Linacre House, Jordan Hill, Oxford OX2 8DP, UK
30 Corporate Drive, Suite 400, Burlington, MA 01803, USA

First published 2005
Revised edition 2009

British Library Cataloguing in Publication Data
A catalogue record for this book is available from the British Library

Library of Congress Cataloging-in-Publication Data
A catalog record for this book is available from the Library of Congress

ISBN 978-0-08-055747-2

For information on all Elsevier Butterworth-Heinemann publications
visit our website at www.elsevierdirect.com

Printed and bound in Hungary

Contents

Activities

Figures

Tables

Series preface

Whether you are a tutor/trainer or studying management development to further your career, Management Extra provides an exciting and flexible resource helping you to achieve your goals. The series is completely new and up-to-date, and has been written to harmonise with the 2004 national occupational standards in management and leadership. It has also been mapped to management qualifications, including the Institute of Leadership & Management's middle and senior management qualifications at Levels 5 and 7 respectively on the revised national framework.

For learners, coping with all the pressures of today's world, Management Extra offers you the flexibility to study at your own pace to fit around your professional and other commitments. Suddenly, you don't need a PC or to attend classes at a specific time – choose when and where to study to suit yourself! And, you will always have the complete workbook as a quick reference just when you need it.

For tutors/trainers, Management Extra provides an invaluable guide to what needs to be covered, and in what depth. It also allows learners who miss occasional sessions to 'catch up' by dipping into the series.

This series provides unrivalled support for all those involved in management development at middle and senior levels.

Reviews of Management Extra

I have utilised the Management Extra series for a number of Institute of Leadership and Management (ILM) Diploma in Management programmes. The series provides course tutors with the flexibility to run programmes in a variety of formats, from fully facilitated, using a choice of the titles as supporting information, to a tutorial based programme, where the complete series is provided for home study. These options also give course participants the flexibility to study in a manner which suits their personal circumstances. The content is interesting, thought provoking and up-to-date, and, as such, I would highly recommend the use of this series to suit a variety of individual and business needs.

Martin Davies BSc(Hons) MEd CEngMIMechE MCIPD FITOL FInstLM
Senior Lecturer, University of Wolverhampton Business School

At last, the complete set of books that make it all so clear and easy to follow for tutor and student. A must for all those taking middle/senior management training seriously.

Michael Crothers, ILM National Manager

Information is crucial

Information is so crucial to all aspects of our lives that we literally cannot afford to manage it badly. Individuals and organisations rely on their ability to select and process information, both to make sense of their local environment and to try to understand the bigger picture. Information management underpins the key activities of planning, analysis, action and, above all, learning and development.

How to make information useful

Organisations need to manage information well and consistently in order to be responsive to the needs of their customers. This book approaches information management from two key perspectives:

◆ How you as a manager use and manage information

◆ The information management process and how it impacts on decision making and organisational performance.

It looks at information in five themes, starting with the sourcing of information and culminating in an exploration of the ways in which organisations manage information and knowledge.

Finding information to meet your needs –
finding good sources of information

Managing your incoming information –
reducing the overload

Managing your outgoing information –
the way you communicate information

How organisations manage information and knowledge –
the systems

How organisations manage information and knowledge –
the content

Your objectives are to:

◆ Identify sources of information relevant to your needs inside and outside of your organisation

◆ Evaluate and improve the quality of your information sources

◆ Learn how to manage information overload

◆ Describe key principles for communicating effectively in writing

◆ Identify the principles behind information system design and management

◆ Explain the features of knowledge management.

1 Information and decision making

People need information to plan their work, meet their deadlines and achieve their goals. They need it to analyse problems and make decisions. Information is certainly not in short supply these days, but not all of it is useful or reliable. This first theme explores your needs for information and asks you to consider how they are served by the sources of information that are available to you.

In this theme you will:

◆ **Consider the differences between data, information and knowledge**

◆ **Identify and evaluate the sources of information that you use**

◆ **Assess whether information flows effectively within your team and identify areas for improvement**

◆ **Analyse how effectively you use the Internet as an information source.**

From data to information to knowledge and learning

H D Clifton (1990) wrote that 'one man's information is another man's data', and certainly the definitions are blurred. However, it is now generally agreed that 'data' is pure and unprocessed – facts and figures without any added interpretation or analysis. Depending on the context, data can be highly significant. Think of a cricket or football score, your name and address. Since it provides the raw material to build information, it also has to be accurate. Any inaccuracies within the initial raw data will magnify as they aggregate upwards, and will seriously corrupt the validity of any conclusions you draw from it or decisions you base upon it.

Data

In a business context, data is associated with the operational aspects of the business and its day-to-day running. As such, it is often entered into a system and stored in large quantities, for example payroll data and sales figures. Such input data goes to create a data 'set' – names and addresses for a mail-merge file, an index to an online product database. It has to be structured correctly – all systems have some kind of validation process to check for obvious technical errors and missing data. To be reliable, the content needs to be accurate, not simply in terms of the correct number and type of characters per data field, but what the data actually represents in terms of meaning. This needs human intervention. Another aspect that affects accuracy is where the data comes from. You may be able to check your own in-house sources – for example, for internally generated data such as the payroll – but have to depend on trust (or the reputation of the supplier) for data received from outside, for example customer credit card details.

Information

So how does 'data' (whether internal or external) become 'information'? When it is applied to some purpose and is adding value which has meaning for the recipient, for example taking sets of sales figures (data) and producing a sales report on them (information).

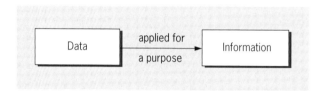

Figure 1.1 *From data to information*

Of course, the same set of data can be used to produce different kinds of information, depending on how it is applied and who applies it. The same sales figures that you use to produce a market sector report might be used by someone else to justify adding to or reducing the size of the sales team. Such information can be used to manage a department, and for short and medium-term planning. Data can move to information and be turned to practical advantage very quickly – in 1815 the London Stock Market rapidly took advantage of the news brought by carrier pigeon of Wellington's victory at Waterloo, which arrived two days before the human messenger arrived.

Information produced inside the organisation can be supplemented by a wealth of business information produced outside – market analyses, reports and case studies, for example.

> Put briefly, information by itself is only of use if it is:
> - the right information (fit for the purpose)
> - at the right time
> - in the right format
> - at the right price.

Knowledge

Just as the words 'data' and 'information' are used interchangeably, there is considerable blurring and confusion between the terms 'information' and 'knowledge'. It is helpful to think of knowledge as being of two types: the instinctive, subconscious, tacit or hidden knowledge, and the more formal, explicit or publicly available knowledge. An everyday example of these might be the knowledge that you use when driving a car (tacit), compared with the knowledge available from a driving manual or the Highway Code (explicit).

Theme 5 looks at knowledge in more detail and how it can be managed within organisations.

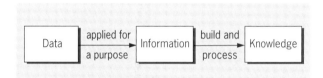

Figure 1.2 *From data to information to knowledge*

In a business context, knowledge is often linked to strategic levels of management and long-term business planning, where it is associated with having a head for business or business flair. However, knowledge vital to an organisation's success can come from any level within it, and needs to be recognised as an important part of organisational assets. It combines information, experience and insight into a mix that is unique to every employee. It is this mix of understandings, based on personal knowledge at a tacit level, that creates the strengths and at times the vulnerability of organisations. It is important for organisations to recognise that holding knowledge at the tacit or hidden level can only have value where people are isolated from everyone else in their decision making. This is neither realistic nor good business practice.

Let's sum up data–information–knowledge with an everyday example. Assume that you're trying to decide on a specialist holiday for photography enthusiasts. Here, very broadly, are the stages you will go through:

Stage 1: collect lots of brochures on photography holidays. This is your basic data store.

Stage 2: work through the brochures, filtering out what you don't want by applying your own criteria to them. Some will be in places you don't want to go to, or at the wrong time of year, or the programmes may be at the wrong level of expertise (you may be looking for some advanced tuition, and many of the holidays are geared to beginners). You can now apply your information and make a decision on where to go on your holiday.

3

Stage 3: you go on your holiday and build your knowledge from testing your actual experience of the holiday against the information you had when you booked it. This knowledge (which you can use next time you want a similar holiday) can be kept to yourself (tacit) or you can share it by reporting back to your local photography club (explicit).

Capitalising on knowledge by making the tacit explicit, and identifying and managing the processes that nurture it, is a thread that runs through this book.

Building knowledge – learning

So how do we collect, process and build our knowledge? Kolb (1985) believes that there are four stages we all go through as part of the learning cycle:

♦ learning from feeling (through specific experience and relations with other people)

♦ learning by watching and listening (looking at things from different perspectives, observing carefully and reflecting before making judgements)

♦ learning by thinking (reflecting on and analysing ideas, drawing up mental maps and planning)

♦ learning by doing (getting things done, influencing other people, taking risks).

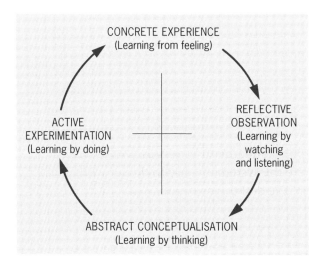

Figure 1.3 *Kolb's learning cycle*   Source: *Kolb* (1985)

We all go through each of these processes to an extent, but different people feel more comfortable with some than with others. For example, an action-oriented person who likes to learn by doing may get very frustrated in a learning-by-watching situation or in one that requires reflection and analysis. It is useful for managers to be aware of their own and their staff's learning styles, since these provide valuable insights into making most effective use of different methods of training.

Argyris and Schön (1974) argue that people act in accordance with a set of mental maps that they themselves have created. It is these subconscious maps (or private, self-generated theories) that guide people's actions. They called these theories that are implicit in what we do theories-in-use: these are what govern our actual behaviour. The words we use to describe that behaviour to others – how we like to justify our actions to other people, or what we would like them to think – can be quite different. This is called espoused theory. It may sound cynical, but if someone asks you how you would behave in a particular set of circumstances, the answer you will give will almost certainly be espoused theory: the public rather than the private set of principles.

Argyris and Schön's view is that real effectiveness results from developing congruence between theory-in-use and espoused theory: creating harmony between your inner and outer self.

Theme 5 looks at a theory-in-use model and the options for organisational learning.

Learning – from the individual to the organisation

People learn by seeking out information when faced with a new situation, and using this information to draw conclusions and form mental models which they use as the basis for their action. If these mental models are confirmed and reinforced by our experience in reality, then over time they become so familiar that they become routine, used automatically and with no conscious effort.

This applies to the presenter who always opens up proceedings with a joke. It also applies to the air traffic controller at an international airport, but in this case we expect the knowledge to be embedded and made explicit through a series of rules and procedures that are recognised and shared by everyone else.

Organisations use routines, rules and procedures as a way of sharing knowledge and creating standardised processes throughout the organisation. These are the systems we use to do our work. Such systems existed before the desktop computer, but computerisation has led to sophisticated information technology (IT) systems for accessing, inputting, processing and sharing information that can be used widely and quickly across the organisation.

The problem for organisations is that routines become old learning and so embedded into our systems that they stifle creativity and the flexibility to respond to changing circumstances. This flexibility – the ability to change and learn – is essential to organisations if they are to survive and grow. The way organisations seek to encourage learning and the sharing of information and knowledge are important aspects of information management.

Activity 1
Identify the differences between data and information

Objectives

This activity will help you to:

◆ check your understanding of data, information and knowledge

◆ identify how you add value to data and information to serve your purpose and create knowledge.

Task

1 List six items of data or information that you receive regularly.

2 Categorise each as 'data' or 'information'.

3 Summarise what you use each item for – your purpose.

4 Note how you add value to each item to create information or knowledge.

5 Who is involved in this process?

Item of data/ information?	Data or information	Purpose	How you add value	Who is involved in adding value?

Feedback

Your work on this activity should have given you some insight into the fact that data on its own is of limited value, and that value has to be added to it to turn it into information. However, the key value-added is knowledge. Use this activity to gain a deeper appreciation of the knowledge available in yourself and your colleagues.

Information comes in many forms

Here are just a few reasons why you, as a manager, need information:

♦ You need to understand what the organisation as a whole is doing, as well as understand what is happening in your own unit or department

♦ You need to be aware of wider industry developments that may impact on the business

♦ It helps day-to-day problem solving and longer-term planning

♦ It can avoid having to reinvent the wheel

♦ Being aware of different practices and other ways of doing things can spark off new ideas and facilitate change.

You use information all the time, often unconsciously. It comes in many different forms, and these are explained here.

Forms of information

Forms of information include the following:

♦ **Internal and external** – information generated inside the organisation and information generated outside. External intelligence and research may be incorporated into internal reports, and issues arising from internal reports may stimulate external market research.

Information need not be written down or be verbalised to be valuable

♦ **Electronic and hard copy (paper-based), and spoken.** At Sun Microsystems, employees receive, on average, 100 e-mails each day, but few people work in a paperless office. Most people also use conversation with others for information.

◆ **Hard and soft** – or quantitative and qualitative. Hard information is often derived from large quantities of precise factual data, such as figures, that lends themselves to statistical analysis. Soft information, on the other hand, tends to come from few sources and depends on opinions, feelings, impressions and judgements.

◆ **Formal and informal.** This is worth exploring in more depth.

Formal and informal

Some of the **formal** information sources you might use every day include:

◆ newspapers or electronic newsfeeds

◆ magazine articles

◆ management reports

◆ staff disciplinary procedures

◆ videos of product presentations

◆ layouts, maps, blueprints.

You will also use a number of **informal** information sources – so informal that you might not even recognise them as such! They can include:

◆ a chat with the managing director's personal assistant whilst queuing for lunch

◆ checking out a problem with a colleague

◆ meeting up with colleagues from the same trade or professional association at the annual conference

◆ informal contacts with suppliers and customers.

Some of the most useful of these sources will be information gatekeepers – people who routinely collect, evaluate and disseminate information in an informal way which may have nothing to do with their job role. These people are well aware of the way information flows around their local environment, and can exercise an influence that goes well beyond their notional status within the organisation.

If you think about it, information need not even be written down or verbalised to be valuable. You can learn a lot about an organisation and its culture simply by walking about and keeping your eyes open, observing the way the organisation goes about its business and presents itself to staff and the outside world.

There are some key differences in the characteristics of formal and informal information sources, as shown in Table 1.1.

Formal	Informal
Available to more than one person	May be an interchange between just two people
Information captured has been recorded in some way, so can be reused	The information is transient – not stored or retrievable
The information used is selected by the recipient – for example, you decide which newspaper reports you are going to read	The information is selected by the provider
Information tends to be static	Information is interactive
Information is likely to conform to the organisation's promoted self-image – it is likely to be 'espoused theory'	Information is more likely to be 'private' and although partial, is likely to be closer to theory-in-use than formal information sources

Table 1.1 *Characteristics of formal and informal information sources*

There are several reasons why managers prefer informal to formal methods of information transfer:

◆ The response and feedback is instant. The whole process is quicker and so is perceived as more efficient (even if the information is only patchy or actually inaccurate).

◆ Being personal, it is targeted at the recipient, so some initial filtering will have been carried out (but is this the half of the picture you want and need...?).

◆ They might not know what useful formal information is available, or how to access it.

◆ Cultural reasons: decisions are often made on the basis of experience and judgement, not painstaking fact finding.

In practice, it makes sense to use a mix of formal and informal, hard and soft data to get a complete picture.

Table 1.2 shows some typical information needs and the information sources that might meet them.

Need/purpose	Types of information	
Produce a report on ice-cream sales for June	Who asked for the report and who will read it Projected and actual sales figures Previous year's figures Meteorological data Report of June launch of new ice-cream product by major competitor	
Your awareness of your own organisational environment (keeping your finger on the pulse)	Company reports and budgets Products and services launched or axed Internal newsletters and memos Meetings	Discussions at the coffee machine Share price Competitor share price
Competitor intelligence	Press reports on company performance and activities Market research data/market analysis Company websites Company annual reports	Trade journals News reports Share price Trends analysis and forecasting Industry gossip

Table 1.2 *Examples of information needs and sources*

Activity 2
Categorise information sources

Objective

Use this activity to analyse the different kinds of information you use on a regular basis.

Task

1 In the first column in the chart provided, note down eight information sources that you use on a regular basis.

2 Categorise them as formal or informal, internal or external, electronic, hard copy or verbal, hard (factual) or soft (impressionistic or qualitative).

3 Score them for usefulness on a scale of 1 to 5, where 1 is low usefulness and 5 is high usefulness.

4 Identify your three most useful sources, and analyse why these are the most useful.

Information source	Formal or informal	Internal or external	Electronic, hard copy or verbal	Hard or soft	Usefulness 1 = low 5 = high
					☐ ☐ ☐ ☐ ☐ 1 2 3 4 5
					☐ ☐ ☐ ☐ ☐ 1 2 3 4 5
					☐ ☐ ☐ ☐ ☐ 1 2 3 4 5
					☐ ☐ ☐ ☐ ☐ 1 2 3 4 5
					☐ ☐ ☐ ☐ ☐ 1 2 3 4 5
					☐ ☐ ☐ ☐ ☐ 1 2 3 4 5
					☐ ☐ ☐ ☐ ☐ 1 2 3 4 5
					☐ ☐ ☐ ☐ ☐ 1 2 3 4 5

Three best sources	Analysis

Feedback

You may have found that you mainly use informal and electronic data, largely because it's accessible, or that you have a definite preference for hard data as it gives you the facts. Build on this activity by considering whether you are making full use of all the sources that might be useful for your purpose. For example, if you tend to use hard data, think about whether seeking opinions may give you different, valuable perspectives. Think about how you can improve the usefulness of the sources, for example, can you be clearer about what you want from the source? See also Theme 2: *Evaluating information*.

Information as an aid to decision making

Much decision making is based on our inbuilt mental models and knowledge base, but this tacit information source can be corroborated and enhanced by formal decision-support mechanisms.

The decision-making process

How do *you* make decisions? Do you assemble all the facts relating to the problem? Rely on your experience and insight? Shut your eyes and hope for the best? Most people do some or all of these things at different times, depending on the nature of the decision. However, the decision-making process shown in Figure 1.4 describes the basic steps involved in consciously making a decision.

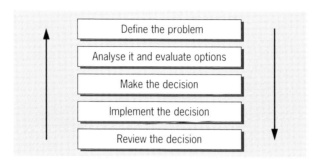

Figure 1.4 *The decision-making process*

The key step is the second one: analyse and evaluate options. Whatever the problem – sorting out a production schedule, conducting a staff appraisal, negotiating a deal – you will need either consciously or unconsciously to weigh up the situation and make decisions accordingly.

An increasing difficulty facing managers now is the speed at which these decisions have to be made: there is just no time for detailed investigation. In an age when managers are faced with more and more information, there is less and less time in which to evaluate its usefulness. As a result, decisions are made on the basis of partial information, wrong information – or whatever information is *available*, rather than *appropriate*.

The concept of cause and effect is commonly used in the way people argue and reason. In making our choices, it is important to identify the right causes and effects – it is all too easy to focus on the symptoms rather than the root causes. It is also necessary to consider your decision-making criteria – what you want to achieve, within what time frame, with what resources. This does assume, of course, that there is a single 'right' decision that you can make to achieve a predictable, successful outcome.

Informix, a software development company, carried out a survey in 1999 to examine how decisions are made in different organisations around the world, and to find out how well the available information, in all its forms, supported the decision-making process. A general finding was that managers, even when they are supported by a multitude of different information sources, find decision making extremely stressful. Most of these managers quoted examples of major decisions that were made incorrectly in the previous six months, and the larger the organisation, the more likely it was to have had a problem.

One of the most important detrimental factors affecting decision making was limited, incorrect or misinterpreted data.

Some key findings of the survey:

◆ 32 per cent of the sample had made an important business decision in the past six months based on hope or luck

◆ the single biggest cause of stress in decision making is a lack of information

◆ 33 per cent of managers ignore relevant data either when making a decision in the first place or when it becomes apparent that a decision has been incorrect.

Source: *Informix* (1999)

What happens when it goes wrong? Below are some examples of information disasters, where the information needed to make decisions was unavailable or ignored:

◆ On 19 October 1987, the Dow Jones Industrial Average took its biggest one-day plunge in the history of the US Stock Market. A major factor in this was that information systems malfunctioned and impeded information flows.

◆ In the same month, British meteorologists failed to appreciate the strength of the oncoming winds which led to one of the biggest storms in living memory: they ignored the available information.

◆ Nuclear scientists at Three Mile Island, and later Chernobyl, failed to take account quickly enough of the information coming from their instrumentation to prevent accidents happening.

Catastrophes of all manner can and do ensue because of what the behavioural scientist might call 'dysfunctional information attitudes and behaviours'. This is a fancy phrase that means that information has been mismanaged somehow, somewhere, by someone, at some time, and often with disastrous consequences in terms of human misery, political misfortune or business failure.

Source: *Horton and Lewis* (1991)

Let's look more closely at the kinds of decision making in which managers are involved.

Levels of management decisions

Management decisions are made at three broad levels within the organisation, and each type of decision has its own characteristics:

Operational decisions: these are the day-to-day decisions affecting the running of the organisation. The decisions tend to be short term (days or weeks) and need to be made quite frequently. For example, a supermarket deciding on whether it needs to order more strawberries to cope with current demand.

Tactical decisions: these have a longer time frame (months or years) and tend to be made by middle managers who are directly involved in implementing the policies of the organisation. For example, a toy shop timing the start of its Christmas promotion.

Strategic decisions: these are made by top management, and since they affect the organisational plans of the whole business, possibly for a number of years, they are not made very frequently. For example, whether to sell off a subsidiary company in response to falling profits.

All these decisions will require information, but the type of information that is needed will be different for each level of decision making. See Figure 1.5.

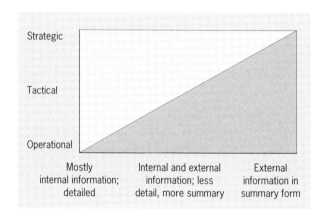

Figure 1.5 *Characteristics of information for management decisions*

Source: *Nickerson* (2001)

Operational decisions rely mostly on internal, detailed data: how many strawberries did we sell yesterday, or last weekend? **Tactical** decisions involve a wider spread of less detailed information: for the past two years, what were the sales figures for the month prior to the Christmas promotion and during the promotion? **Strategic** decisions may use long-term performance figures from inside the organisation, but also financial forecasts and analyses from the wider marketplace, its own shareholders' views, and so on.

Cross-functional, in-house systems such as accounting, finance, marketing and human resources (HR) can, of course, support decision making at every level of the organisation, whether operational, tactical or strategic. There are also general *types* of information systems for management support, which we will look at a little later in this section.

Getting the right information to make decisions

In an ideal world, getting the right information to make decisions would be very easy. We would just type a question into our PC, or know exactly the right person we need to telephone in order to get an instant, accurate and authoritative answer.

In real life, most of us have to get by without perfect one-stop solutions. Where do we get the information we need to make decisions when our systems are not organisation wide, but are locked into 'silos' where we can perhaps drill down to increasing levels of detail, but not across to the vital missing piece of data that is held within another department?

If you think of a decision you have made recently and about where the information came from, you will probably realise that it is a mix of your own knowledge, whatever information was available and maybe a chat to a couple of colleagues who always seem to have an answer or know where to find one. Think a little more broadly: how does your team get the information it needs in order to operate? The model would probably look something like the one shown in Figure 1.6.

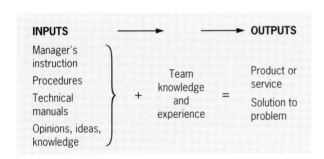

Figure 1.6 *Information for team operations*

In this model, the inputs (your basic raw materials) come from a diverse mix of sources. Some of these will be formal, some very informal – but no less valuable for that. These inputs will be processed by individuals or the team to produce the desired outputs (a specific product or service, or the solution to a problem). Getting it right assumes that the flow of information, both formal and informal, is:

◆ unimpeded – there are no bottlenecks and blockages (human or technical)

◆ able to move upwards, downwards and sideways with equal ease

◆ equally accessible to all who need it.

An organisational approach to take some of the luck out of getting the right information for decision making – for making individual knowledge explicit and sharing it across the organisation – is to develop formal information systems to support managers.

Formal information systems for management support

Computer systems that can store and manipulate information provide a structured and accessible support for management decision making. Here are descriptions of three kinds of systems in common use: management information systems (MIS), decision support systems (DSS) and executive support systems (ESS).

Management information systems (MIS)

A management information system, or MIS, supports management decisions by providing information in the form of reports and responses to queries to managers at different levels within an organisation. The MIS database that provides the information to the manager comes from both inside and outside the organisation, much of it from the data stored in transaction processing systems – the nuts and bolts of day-to-day operations and processes.

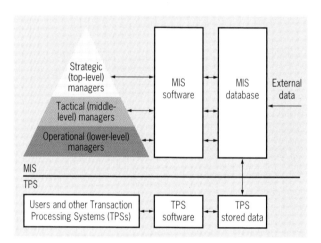

Figure 1.7 *Structure of an MIS*   Source: *Nickerson* (2001)

Decision support systems (DSS)

Whereas an MIS provides information from a database with little or no analysis, a decision support system (DSS) helps managers by analysing data from a database and providing them with the results, often in the form of statistical calculations or mathematical models. It is used most often for decisions at tactical and strategic levels. The main system components are the DSS database that contains the data, and the model base which contains the mathematical models and statistical calculation routines that are used to analyse data from the database. Decision support systems are often used in situations where decisions are unstructured or semi-structured, and are good for working through 'what if' scenarios to calculate the effects of different decisions on outcomes (what happens if we start the Christmas promotion two weeks earlier?)

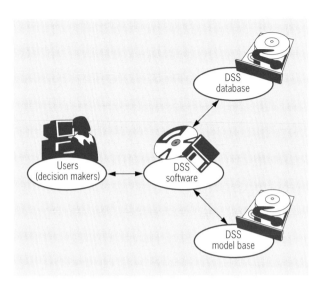

Figure 1.8 *Structure of a DSS* Source: *Nickerson* (2001)

A variation on this is a group DSS, typically used in a networked environment where several PCs are joined together, in which users can collaborate to reach a group decision.

Executive support systems (ESS)

Also known as executive information systems, these are designed to support strategic business decisions. Although strategic decisions usually involve summarised information, there is often a need for a specific level of detail to pinpoint a particular problem. For example, executives in an organisation that is thinking of selling off a failing subsidiary might want to try to discover where its failure lies: is it a particular market segment, a region, a product line? This will often require a drilling-down process to get from general information to highly specific data subsets.

The user of an ESS will typically need to access a wide variety of databases: internal, external, those created by the individual user and electronic mailboxes.

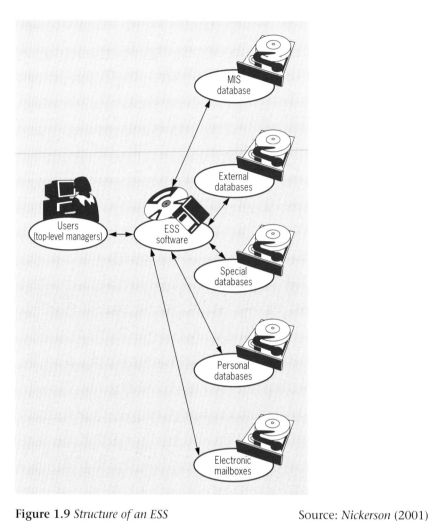

Figure 1.9 *Structure of an ESS*   Source: *Nickerson* (2001)

Other systems

Increasingly, managers are looking at more sophisticated methods such as **expert systems** that mimic the way a human would analyse a situation and recommend a particular course of action, and **knowledge management systems** that can organise, store and enable shared access to the collective knowledge of the organisation.

The point to remember about all of these systems is that the quality of the output is only as good as the quality of the input.

The activities that follow explore the theme of information flows and systems for management support. You will start by looking at your information sources.

Activity 3
Explore information for decision making

Objective

Use this activity to assess whether you have the appropriate information you need to make decisions.

Task

1 Think of a decision you need to make in your work at the moment or in the near future. Write this at the top of the table provided.

2 What information do you believe is essential for you to make a well-informed decision? List the information in the first column.

3 In the second column, note down where you think you can find this information – who has this information, what form is it in?

4 In the final column, assess whether you can get access to each piece of information to help you to make your decision. If it is available, is it in a form that you can use?

5 What are the implications of the availability of the information on the quality of your decision?

Decision:		
Information required	Source?	Can you access it?

Implications for quality of the decision:

Feedback

Managers rarely have access to all the information they need to make good decisions. You may well have found that the right kind of information is available, but not when you need it or in a form that you can use. However, the decisions still have to be made, in spite of gaps in the information or contradictory information.

You have to bring your judgement and experience to bear when making a decision based on incomplete information. You often have to make assumptions based on an unclear situation. Be aware of any limitations in the information used to make a decision so that you know how 'safe' the decision is likely to be. By doing this, you can take corrective action quickly if new information comes to light.

You may find Theme 2 on information overload and evaluating information helpful in improving your use of information for decision making.

Activity 4
Plot information flows within your team

Objective

This activity will help you to identify the way information flows around your team.

Task

1 Select a key process or activity carried out by team members. It could be one that you or your team believes is not working very well.

2 Answer the following questions about the activity and record your responses in the chart provided.

  ◆ What are the main steps involved in this activity? (Note the decisions, actions or outputs.)

  ◆ Who is involved at each step? (List the team members who carry out each step and who need to be kept informed at each step.)

  ◆ What information is needed to carry out each step? (There may be a need for several items of information in different forms.)

  ◆ Where does this information come from? (It may come from a customer, from someone else within the team or from another part of the organisation.)

  ◆ Who receives this information? (List the person or people who receive the information.)

◆ What does that person do with the information? (For example store it, use it to carry out the step, pass it on to another person, use it for another purpose unrelated to the step.)

3   Now review your responses. You may want to do this with your team. Do team members have the information they need for each step? Does the information go to the right people?

Process/activity: Steps	Who is involved	Info needed	Source	Who receives	Action taken

Feedback

This activity may have given you some insights into the way information flows around your unit/department for one particular process/activity. In an ideal world, the flow of information would be clearly related to its purpose. However, you may have identified practices such as information short cuts (which bypass people who need to know), toing and froing of requests or problems, or a heavy concentration of a small number of key people who are involved in information transactions whether they need to be or not. Use the activity to clarify information needs and regularise gaps or other deficiencies.

Activity 5
Specify an information system for management support

Objective

Use this activity to clarify the kind of decision support that you would like to see from an information system.

Task

Assume that you can specify and purchase an information system to help you in your job.

1 Think about the features you would like an information system to have in order to give you the most benefit in terms of making it easier for you to do your job to a high standard. In the chart provided, note these features and the benefits they would bring.

2 In the third column, tick the features/benefits that are already available to support you in your current information system.

Features	Benefits – how each feature would help you do your work	Already available?
		☐
		☐
		☐
		☐
		☐

3 Now think about which of the following types of information system would best be able to give you the features you require.

♦ Management information system?

♦ Decision support system?

♦ Executive support system?

Which system will best provide the required features, and why?

Feedback

Working on this activity should highlight any weaknesses in your existing support structure or the need for a more sophisticated information system. Consult with colleagues in your IT department to see whether any of your identified improvements can be implemented.

Using the Web as an information resource

Here we provide some very practical guidance on finding the information you need, both to make informed decisions and to build up your own knowledge base in your chosen area. It will not eliminate all the problems involved in finding Web-based material, but should give you some sharper tools to help you along the way.

Search engines

Note that although the World Wide Web is technically only a part of the Internet, it is the one that is most familiar to most people, and the terms 'Web' and 'Internet' are used interchangeably.

The starting point for all Web searches is a **search engine** – quite literally, a force that responds to an information request by searching the Web for what it interprets as relevant material. Search engines are also referred to here as **indexes** as they act like gigantic indexes to selected chunks of the Web. They take an input search word (**search term**) or phrase, and retrieve a set of results (**hits**) that relate to that term or phrase from the Web pages that they have identified, collected into a virtual database and indexed. Note the word 'selected' – none of them scans absolutely everything, and you

If you're looking for non-English language search engines, try Searchengine Colossus (www.searchenginecolossus.com) which covers about 100 countries.

Activity 6
Use the Web for research

Objectives

If you are not experienced in using the Web for research, use this activity to:

♦ practise using the Web to find the information you need

♦ consider how far the Web can help you to carry out aspects of your job.

Task

1 You are going to Paris this coming weekend. Use the Web to find out:

♦ whether you will need to take an umbrella with you (the answer is not that you will buy an umbrella when you get there)

♦ the current rate of exchange.

Keep a note of how long it takes you to find this information.

2 How do you think the Web will help in your work and in your development programme? Write your thoughts below.

How the Web will help in my work and development programme:

Feedback

1 How successful you were, and how quickly you found the information, will partly depend on which search engine you began with. Finding a five-day weather forecast is fairly straightforward, but you might have had to work a bit harder to get at the exchange rate.

2 Your response here is likely to depend on the nature of your work, and how successfully you are currently using the Web to find information. Some people find the Web frustrating and slow to use at first. The quality of websites can also cause problems if they are not user-friendly.

Although the following is not a comprehensive list, if you need to do any of these activities as part of your work, you should find the Web helpful:

- ◆ Track and keep up to date with news events – including business news and share prices

- ◆ Find out government trends or statistics

- ◆ Get government guidelines on matters affecting business, for example employment law, the introduction of the euro, quality in business

- ◆ Find out about management theory, models and techniques

- ◆ Find bibliographic information

- ◆ Check out competitor information

- ◆ Research supplier companies

- ◆ Find new employees

- ◆ Find out what non-governmental organisations are doing.

Some organisations also use the Internet for business-to-business commerce. It becomes a marketplace.

Find out whether your organisation has a policy about using the Internet at work for research. Some organisations, concerned about inappropriate access to the Web at work, restrict or monitor its use.

◆ Recap

Consider the differences between data, information and knowledge

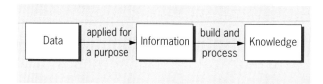

◆ Information may be:

– electronic, hard copy or verbal

– quantitative or qualitative.

Identify and evaluate the sources of information that you use

◆ Information sources may be:

– Internal or external

– Formal or informal.

◆ Managers often prefer informal sources because the data is instantly available, but using a mix of hard and soft information from formal and informal sources is a more reliable foundation for decision making. As a manager, you need to cultivate a range of information sources to meet your needs.

◆ The information you need depends to a large extent on the types of decisions you make. Operational decisions can be made on the basis of internal data whereas strategic decisions require data and analyses from external sources.

Assess whether information flows effectively within your team and identify areas for improvement

◆ Analysing the flow of information into your team may reveal blockages or bottlenecks, or that some people cannot access the information they need. This provides a basis for improving operational processes and decision making.

◆ Computer systems are used to improve the flow of information. The different levels of decision making are supported by three types of system: management information systems, decision support systems and executive support systems.

Analyse how effectively you use the Internet as an information source

◆ The four main types of search tool are: free text search engines, human-generated indexes, metasearch tools and natural language search enagines.

◆ Choosing the right search engine and developing your knowledge of advanced search techniques will increase your efficiency and improve your search results.

 **More @**

Wilson, D. (2002) *Managing Information: IT for Business Process*, **Butterworth-Heinemann**
This book describes how successful organisations make best use of information and knowledge and explains why information technology is essential for the management of business processes.

Argyris, C. (1999) *On Organisational Learning*, **Blackwell Publishers**
This book for managers and development specialists provides more on double loop learning and how organisations evolve and learn. Try also www.infed.org/thinkers/argyris.htm for an overview of Argyris's work.

Buckley, P. and Clark, D. (2004) *A Rough Guide to the Internet*, **Rough guides**
Written in plain English, this book covers everything from getting online for the first time to advanced tips and tricks.

Information Week at www.informationweek.com and **BetterManagement** at www.bettermanagement.com are both useful sites to search for downloadable articles, white papers and research reports.

> Research published shows that companies risk wasting their investment in technology implemented to manage information because they are failing to tackle the 'human hurdle' – up to two thirds of respondents had problems with information overload, employees not having time to share knowledge and reinventing the wheel.

Source: *Information Management Report* (2000)

So, we're getting more information, more rapidly, from more sources, in more formats – and less and less time to deal with it.

Activity 7
Assess the extent of your information overload

Objective

Use this activity to assess how far you are overloading yourself with unnecessary information.

Task

Fill in the following questionnaire by ticking all the statements that apply to you.

I often collect more information than I need in case I miss out on something vital	☐
I need to gather a lot of information to keep myself well informed	☐
I need a lot of information to justify the decisions I make	☐
I often collect information in case it might come in handy in the future	☐
I have to get on lots of people's 'cc' lists so that I know what's going on	☐
I have to collect a lot of information so that I can cross-check its validity	☐
I find that my searches for information often produce a lot of irrelevant data	☐

Feedback

There are no 'right' answers, but your work on this activity might have given you pause for thought. You may like to consider:

◆ Are there other, better ways of keeping up to date?

◆ Can I improve my searching and information retrieval skills?

◆ Should I be more confident in my decision making?

Evaluating information

For our decision making to be quality decision making, the information that supports it needs to be quality information. But what does 'quality' actually mean in this context? How can we recognise and measure it? What criteria or benchmarks can we use? One difficulty is that, over time, the quantitative and qualitative value of information can decay. Also, information quality in this context can be considered from the point of view of function (does it do what it is meant to do and what are the functions it satisfies or supports?) or of form (the image or intangible benefits that accrue from having the information).

What's the added value?

For some experts, the problem of information overload is to a great extent part of a failure to create 'quality' information – that is, information that has real value-added content. This of course assumes that you have a very clear idea of what it is that makes a piece of information add value.

Simpson and Prusak (1995) believe that the value of information can only be measured in terms of the benefit you get from using it. But how do you measure this 'benefit in use'? Many approaches have been tried but none has stood the test of real-time business practice, and yet individuals try to add value in their own communications all the time! Think back to your last couple of conversations. Were any of the people involved:

◆ trying to verify the information given ('Well, you say that, but is it actually true?')

◆ drawing conclusions from the information ('It looks as if what we've got here is...')

◆ challenging something that didn't sound quite right ('Hang on a minute...that can't be right...')?

During these kinds of conversations, although you may not be aware of it, you are evaluating the information you received so that you can work out what to do about it.

From this kind of instinctive evaluation, Simpson and Prusak have devised a model that proposes five universal elements of value in information, shown in Figure 2.1.

Activity 8
Evaluate your incoming information

Objective

Use this activity to evaluate the usefulness of the information you receive in your day-to-day job.

Task

1 In the chart provided, log all the mail (internal, external and e-mail) that you receive in the course of one day.

2 Give each item a score (1 = low and 5 = high) for the universal elements of:

♦ **truth** (your level of confidence in the validity of the information)

♦ **scarcity** (new information or providing new insights)

♦ **guidance** (points the way to action or the diagnosis of a problem)

♦ **accessibility** (availability of information when it is needed and in a form in which you can understand it)

♦ **weight** (relevance or the authority of the sender).

3 From your scores you should be able to see how much of this is 'quality' information and fit for your present purpose.

4 Discuss your findings with colleagues.

Mail item	Truth 1–5	Scarcity 1–5	Guidance 1–5	Accessibility 1–5	Weight 1–5

Mail item	Truth 1–5	Scarcity 1–5	Guidance 1–5	Accessibility 1–5	Weight 1–5

Feedback

Your work on this activity should have given you some ideas about the kinds of information (or informant) that are more (or less) useful to you. Use it to become more selective in your filtering of incoming information.

You should also consider ways to communicate your information needs to those sources that are less than satisfactory. It is possible that small changes can be made that cost very little but make a major difference to the value of that information to you.

Activity 9
Evaluating websites

Objective

Use this activity to explore websites and evaluate their effectiveness.

Task

Evaluate the following websites by rating them from 1 to 5 against each item in the checklist provided. Circle 1 to denote very poor quality; circle 5 to denote very high quality.

BBC – www.bbc.co.uk

McDonald's – www.mcdonalds.com

Singapore Airlines – www.singaporeair.com

	BBC	McDonald's	Singapore Airlines
Purpose of site clear?	1 2 3 4 5	1 2 3 4 5	1 2 3 4 5
Contact details and basic information easy to find?	1 2 3 4 5	1 2 3 4 5	1 2 3 4 5
Coverage appropriate for purpose?	1 2 3 4 5	1 2 3 4 5	1 2 3 4 5
Does the organisation have an established reputation and weight?	1 2 3 4 5	1 2 3 4 5	1 2 3 4 5
Is information likely to be accurate?	1 2 3 4 5	1 2 3 4 5	1 2 3 4 5
Is information current?	1 2 3 4 5	1 2 3 4 5	1 2 3 4 5
Is a site map provided, or is the site easy to navigate?	1 2 3 4 5	1 2 3 4 5	1 2 3 4 5
Is information well presented and arranged?	1 2 3 4 5	1 2 3 4 5	1 2 3 4 5
Does the site compare well with similar organisations?	1 2 3 4 5	1 2 3 4 5	1 2 3 4 5
Are there good help facilities?	1 2 3 4 5	1 2 3 4 5	1 2 3 4 5
Are there links to other sites or supporting materials?	1 2 3 4 5	1 2 3 4 5	1 2 3 4 5
Are these links or supporting materials useful?	1 2 3 4 5	1 2 3 4 5	1 2 3 4 5

Feedback

Discuss your findings with colleagues. Do you share the same general conclusions? Are there any other aspects that you want to evaluate?

Good practice for reducing overload

There is no single tool or technique that will provide a magic answer to all your information overload problems, but there are techniques that can help. Bawden et al. (1999) divide these techniques into **managerial** and **technical**.

Managerial techniques

On the managerial side, a lot of the techniques come under the general heading of time management. You can re-take control of your information by managing your time more effectively, using some of the following techniques:

◆ Structure your information searching more intelligently, and link it directly to your goal: why are you looking for this information, and how can you best find it? This is likely to be quicker and more effective than just surfing in a random way, hoping that something useful will turn up.

◆ Follow the classic time-management recommendation and 'handle a piece of paper only once' (the same applies to electronic messages). Take action on it immediately or delete/ bin it.

◆ Be very selective about the newsgroups and mailing lists you join – they can generate a lot of irrelevant information that is time-consuming to read through.

◆ Delete irrelevant e-mails without reading them.

◆ Only file material when you know it will be difficult to find it again.

◆ Improve your own information literacy – your ability to retrieve, evaluate, organise and use information from a variety of sources. This will include effective management of both paper files and e-mail folders.

All this lies within your own hands. If you are looking at reducing organisation-wide information overload, putting out some sensible rules for e-mail etiquette is a good start. The European Forum for Electronic Business has developed a code of practice to help organisations use e-mail more effectively. Here are some of its main points:

Guidelines for using e-mail

◆ Do you need to e-mail at all? Sometimes it's quicker to telephone.

◆ Give your messages a meaningful title – not 'Meeting' but 'Team meeting 29 April'.

- For clarity (and to save other people's time) restrict action requests to one recipient only, and copy to (cc) anyone else who needs to know.

- Keep your messages brief.

- Don't mail or cc more people that absolutely necessary.

- Think very carefully before putting a message on a distribution list for general use.

- Using the 'BCC' (Blanket Carbon Copy) field instead of 'To' for messages to several people will reduce message size.

- Currency symbols can be changed in transmission. If your e-mails are likely to contain references to different currencies, it's better to use an agreed alpha abbreviation like GBP for sterling and USD for US dollars.

- Use the 'Urgent' flag sparingly, or its impact will be lost.

Source: *Adapted from the European Forum for Electronic Business* (www)

Technical techniques

On the technical side, there are systems for ranking and filtering e-mail and other messages; check for details with your information technology (IT) department. As an individual trying to reduce overload on the Internet, your best approach, as indicated earlier, is to make as much use as you can of personal software agents and any customisation offered by the major search engines.

Activity 10
Use e-mail more effectively

Objective

Use this activity to make more effective use of e-mail.

Task

1   Look at the last 10 e-mails that you received that initiated a dialogue or action (that is, not just responses to e-mails of yours).

2   In the chart provided, note down the message header and sender's initials of one of these e-mails. Then evaluate using the following questions:

- Was it necessary to send this e-mail? (Did you need it? Would a telephone call have been quicker?)

- Is there a meaningful title so you can find it or file it easily? (For example, not 'meeting' but 'Team meeting on 24 Oct'.)

- Was the message sent only to people who need to take action or respond, and were other people copied in ('cc') on a need-to-know basis?

- Is the message brief and to the point?

- Is required action clear?

3   Use the chart below to note down whether each of the messages meets the above e-etiquette guidelines. Write yes, no, or a short comment in each column.

Message header	Sender's initials	E-mail necessary?	Meaningful header?	Appropriate recipients?	Brief and to the point?	Is required action clear?

4   Review your own e-etiquette by using the same criteria. Note down any areas for improvement.

Ways of improving your e-mails:

Feedback

Discuss your work on this activity with colleagues. You may find it helpful to discuss strategies both to deal with a large volume of incoming e-mails and to increase the effectiveness of the ones you send. Would a good-practice checklist for use within the organisation be a good idea?

◆ Recap

Identify information overload and assess why it occurs

◆ When the amount of information received exceeds that desired or needed by a user, it becomes a hindrance and a potential cause of stress, and the user experiences information overload.

◆ Assessing the extent to which you contribute towards your own information overload is a good first step in improving the way you manage and use information.

Evaluate the information you receive by assessing its quality and value to you

◆ Simpson and Prusak (1995) propose that you can evaluate the quality of information available to you using five criteria: **weight** or importance, **truth** or validity, the extent to which you rely on the information for **guidance**, **accessibility** and **scarcity**.

◆ If you are receiving information that is of poor quality, then communicate your needs to your information source to see whether it can be improved.

Reduce your information overload

◆ You can reduce information overload by becoming more selective about the information – including e-mails – that you access and read, and by developing systems for effectively managing hard and soft information.

▶▶ More @

Simpson, C. W. and Prusak, L. (1995), 'Troubles with information overload', *International Journal of Information Management*, Vol. 15, No. 6, 413–425
This is the source article with further information on the Simpson and Prusak model.

Try **Mind Tools** at www.mindtools.com for more on information skills and time management techniques.

3 Communicating information

People handle astonishing quantities of written text on a daily basis, both consciously and unconsciously: newspapers at breakfast, advertising hoardings and shop fronts on the way to work, reports, memos and e-mail on the desktop. They may read a book on the train home, or pick up a few text messages from friends. It is worth pausing for a moment to think about the different ways in which such channels of communication get their message across to you – and what influences how receptive you are to what they are trying to tell you or persuade you to do. How often do you stop reading – simply switch off your attention – from something that is long-winded, difficult to follow, boring or full of errors?

There are lots of very practical reasons why everyone should aim to communicate clearly:

- It makes it easier for the recipient to understand the message, which saves time
- Written instructions that are clear and unambiguous are easy to follow and act upon
- A good written case can be a powerful aid to influencing
- In the case of a dispute (for example a disciplinary case) your written reports may be produced as evidence in an employment tribunal or a court of law
- What you record now may be a precedent that will need to be referred to for guidance in the future
- If the messages aren't understood by the reader, do they count as communication or just a waste of your time and everyone else's?

Many successful business leaders have recognised that the ability to write persuasively – getting people to take their message on board or do what they want them to do – is a key skill. The most effective documents, whether long or short, are those where the author has taken the trouble to ensure maximum impact.

In this theme you will:

- **Identify the features of clear written communication**
- **Evaluate your writing style**
- **Plan an effective presentation**
- **Develop notes and visual aids to support your presentation.**

Planning and structuring your document

You may think that a logical approach is the best way to do this. Surely the facts will speak for themselves? Or perhaps you think that if you really want to get your own way quickly, a bit of coercion will do the trick? Andrew Leigh (1997) believes that learning to develop a persuasive writing style is the best way of encouraging people to accept and endorse what you have to say.

Purpose

An important aspect of this is the purpose of the document, which you need to be absolutely clear about:

- What do you want your readers to do?
- What outcome do you want to achieve?

Readers

An essential step in planning a document is to put yourself in the reader's shoes, and to try to predict how they will understand and react to it. Consider the following questions:

- What do your readers expect to gain by reading your document?
- What length of document will be appropriate for the purpose and the recipient? Are they likely to want a one-page summary or a 10-page analysis?
- How much time will they have to read it?
- What is their likely standpoint on the topic, and how can you counter resistance?
- What questions are they likely to raise?

Since your aim is to communicate with people and persuade them rather than to antagonise them at the outset, it is always useful to start by establishing some common ground and getting across that you understand and respect their position. This is important, even if you then go on to provide evidence that their position is no longer tenable and that they will have to consider changing it.

Structure

You can strengthen whatever case you are making (and this applies to the shortest e-mail or longest report) if you structure a document carefully so that:

- the information in it is prioritised, with the most important information coming first – this will mean giving the 'headlines' and main conclusions first, not leaving the punchline until the end
- you have carefully selected what to include and what to omit – this involves thinking about what information your readers need
- you give some indication of what should or will happen next – in other words your recommendations.

Politeness and clarity will get you a long way. However, there are other means of ensuring that your message is received positively, such as style and tone.

Style and tone

You may not have much leeway with style, as a corporate house style may exist that you have to adhere to. If you are not restricted by a corporate house style, you can make your style more interesting by using active language rather than passive.

Think about the difference between:

- 'It is generally recognised within the company that ...' and
- 'As you know...'

Or the difference between:

- 'The project outline was put together by the author of this document' and
- 'I put the project outline together'.

Keep the language simple and straightforward by avoiding features such as:

- double negatives, for example, 'it was not impossible to foresee the consequences...'
- long words
- a complicated sentence construction
- technical jargon and other features that you may think look professional but in fact just get in the way of understanding and actually lessen the impact of your message.

The aim is to ensure that your reader progresses smoothly through the document, without having to stop and puzzle out what you are trying to say. As well as keeping it simple, it is useful to keep it short, and this may require some discipline and firm editing. Think about how long it takes to unravel a sentence such as the following:

It is our opinion that, in the circumstances, and with all things considered, the best way forward will be to talk initially to HQ, RSB and GRE staff, then JPU, EN and PNU staff about the new procedures and make sure that they are up to date.

If the author of this example is so unconfident about the way ahead, why should you, as the recipient, be convinced? Also, as the recipient, will you instantly recognise all the staff modules referred to? Is it the staff or the procedures that need to be up to date?

Style tips checklist

♦ Avoid long sentences or paragraphs

♦ Use simple, active language

♦ Avoid double negatives

♦ Avoid jargon or overuse of acronyms and abbreviations

♦ Use bullet points and numbered lists to break up the text

♦ Edit ruthlessly – don't hang on to a nice phrase that adds nothing just because you thought of it and like it.

In verbal communication, what you say is often not as important as the way you say it, and the message communicated to the recipient may have little to do with the actual words used. In written communications too, the tone you use may be so inappropriate as to be unacceptable, even if the facts it contains are true. Common errors are being:

♦ aggressive rather than assertive – 'I want this revised and on my desk by 8.30am tomorrow – or else.'

♦ patronising – 'I realise that your experience of this process isn't as extensive as mine. However...'

♦ dismissive – 'This is too trivial to comment on. Just go away and sort it.'

♦ critical – 'That was really stupid.'

Before you send a document, check it by putting yourself in the receiver's shoes. How would you react to being on the receiving end of it?

Other good practice

If the message is clearly set out, does it matter if you make minor errors, break the odd grammatical rule or misspell words? Think about how you would feel if your bank got your name wrong or a brochure for a smart hotel contained basic typing errors. You may feel that these small mistakes undermine the message the company is trying to convey. The key issue here is reliability. The message you receive is that if these people can't take the trouble to get the basics right, what else can't they be bothered to do, and what does that say for their levels of customer care?

These days, most typing and some grammatical errors can be picked up automatically by your spellchecker, but text will still benefit from proofreading to ensure that errors such as 'their' instead of 'there' are corrected, and that all personal names in the document are spelled correctly.

> **Politeness and clarity will get you a long way.**

You also need to keep a lookout for discriminatory language. This pitfall has been around long enough for acceptable alternatives to become current, for example 'workforce' for 'manpower'.

Be careful how you use numerical data in written communications. Incorrect numbers, or statistics provided out of context, can completely undermine your otherwise convincing case.

Presentation

You never get a second chance to make a first impression. If you are preparing a formal report or proposal, take care with the way it is set out and the kind of supporting material it might be useful to include. If, for example, your report contains lots of detailed information that will only be useful to some readers (or, because of its quantity and detail, will actually get in the way of your message) put this in an appendix.

Whatever the length of the document, it should be very easy for the reader to scan through it quickly and get the gist of what it is about. For a short document, that will mean short paragraphs (perhaps numbered) and sub-headings where useful – they will guide the reader quickly through the document content. A longer document requires a greater degree of formality. For a report or proposal, this will mean a title page and table of contents before the body of the document. Don't forget to put a date on it, and if the document will be going through several drafts, give it a version number as well. Make use of headers and footers: they are useful document identifiers, particularly if you have loose sheets in hard copy. Include your own contact details in case any covering letter gets separated from the main document. List appendices in the table of contents.

Sample report format
♦ Title page
♦ Table of contents
♦ Executive summary
♦ Introduction

◆ Methodology and findings

◆ Conclusions and recommendations

◆ Appendices

Activity 11
Evaluate written communications

Objective

This activity will help you to assess the clarity of your written communications.

Task

1 Select a paragraph or two (about 400 words) from a report or long memo that you have written.

2 Evaluate it against the style checklist below, using 1 for a low score and 5 for a high score. What conclusions do you draw from your evaluation?

Style checklist
Does the writer of this text:

◆ avoid long sentences that are difficult to follow?

□ □ □ □ □
1 2 3 4 5

◆ use simple, active language?

□ □ □ □ □
1 2 3 4 5

◆ avoid double negatives?

□ □ □ □ □
1 2 3 4 5

◆ use minimal jargon?

□ □ □ □ □
1 2 3 4 5

◆ use bullet points/lists (when appropriate) to break up the text?

□ □ □ □ □
1 2 3 4 5

◆ use appropriate punctuation, sentence structure and spelling?

□ □ □ □ □
1 2 3 4 5

Conclusions:

3 Now evaluate the following text using the same style checklist below.

> The traffic into London was heavy and it was almost two hours before I parked outside our apartment building. I had thought about it on the way, and I expected him to be there, but seeing him waiting for me as I got out of the car gave me a jolt to the heart. I paused before I crossed the road. He had taken up a position by the entrance where I would have to walk by him. He looked dressed up – black suit, white shirt buttoned to the top, black patent shoes with white flashes. He was staring at me, but his expression told me nothing. I walked towards him quickly, hoping to brush right by him and get indoors, but he stood across my path and I had to stop or push him aside. He looked tense, possibly angry. There was an envelope in his hand.

Source: *McEwan* (1997)

Style checklist
Does the writer of this text:

◆ avoid long sentences that are difficult to follow?   □□□□□ 1 2 3 4 5

◆ use simple, active language?   □□□□□ 1 2 3 4 5

◆ avoid double negatives?   □□□□□ 1 2 3 4 5

◆ use minimal jargon?   □□□□□ 1 2 3 4 5

◆ use bullet points/lists (when appropriate) to break up the text?   □□□□□ 1 2 3 4 5

◆ use appropriate punctuation, sentence structure and spelling?   □□□□□ 1 2 3 4 5

Conclusions:

Feedback

Fiction doesn't always have to be more interesting than fact. A style that is easy to read can be used to catch the reader's interest and sustain it.

Using the power of text in presentations

When you give a presentation, you are formally presenting a problem or a report in a structured way in a face-to-face setting. Just like written documents, a presentation is also an exercise in persuasion, since you are trying to get your audience to accept the message you are delivering to them. You may want them to take a particular course of action as a result of your presentation, or to accept your point of view or modify their own attitudes. Whatever you want from them, it is often the case that your need for their acceptance and approval is greater than their need to hear your message (Jay and Jay, 2000). It makes sense, therefore, for every element of the presentation to help in commanding the audience's attention and in ensuring a positive response to what you have to say.

Planning your presentation

The first element in planning your presentation is to get quite clear what your objective is, and to write this out in one sentence. For example, it might be 'to persuade senior management of the need to review our current customer relationship management system' or 'to present a case for switching resources from product x to product y'. The very fact of having to formulate a written statement will help to clarify exactly what you want, and provide a focus for you to check against as your presentation develops.

Now switch your attention to the audience. How interested, knowledgeable or confrontational are members of your audience likely to be? This will affect the points you want to make and how you propose to put them over. The next steps are as follows:

1   Write down how many sections or topic areas you need to cover, and the key points in each.

2   Note what is really important to get across, and what can be dropped or cut back if there is no time to cover it.

3   Devise some logical order for presenting the different sections. The usual structure is to start with some scene setting, go on to specific issues and end with an indication of what action is required next.

4   Put a notional time allocation against each section.

Did you know...?
Psychologists have plotted the attention span of an audience over a 40-minute period. It starts high, drops quite shallowly for the first 10 minutes, then more steeply until it reaches its lowest point after about 30 minutes. Then, with the end in

sight, it starts to rise again. Make sure you're not making your key point when your audience is at its least receptive!

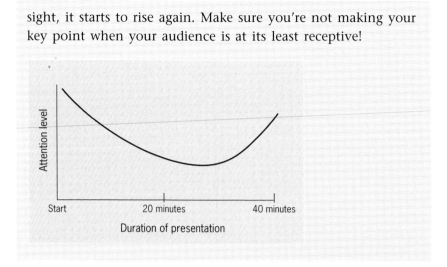

Source: *Jay and Jay* (2000)

Written script or cue cards?

Of course, the very best presenters dispense with notes altogether. They get to their feet or stride onto the podium and hold the audience enthralled with the power of their oratory. Alas, few of us ever achieve this admirable performance. The fact is that spontaneity is hard work, and being a relaxed and engaging presenter requires considerable preparation – not to mention a lot of self-confidence.

Less experienced speakers, or those giving short presentations to colleagues, can use cue cards (small index cards are ideal) on which the main points they want to make (or just key words) are listed. You will still need to prepare (in fact your preparation may need to be even more thorough), but it does mean that you stand a better chance of coming across as natural, and you have the assurance of a discreet written prompt if you suddenly go blank.

If you are a very inexperienced speaker, or the importance or formality of the occasion is one where you just can't afford to fluff your words, a written script can be reassuring. However, unless you're actually giving a lecture, DON'T turn a presentation into one. There is nothing more boring.

All the general principles of good written communication – keep it simple, clear, direct and jargon-free – also apply to a presentation. However, the difference here is that you are speaking not writing, and written and spoken language are very different. The challenge is to make your written script sound as if you are talking through the situation – better to use it as an extended crib rather than slavishly reading out each word.

Preparing notes for a presentation

◆ Use a less grammatical style: 'What are we doing this for?' rather than 'For what purpose are we doing this?'

◆ Write shorter sentences: run a 'comma check' to see whether there are phrases that can be cut altogether or split off to form separate sentences. If you tell your audience, 'Whatever the analysts say, in my opinion, if we go about things in the right way, there is no reason why, by this time next year, we should not come into profit,' you will have them yawning, even if the message is optimistic.

◆ Pose rhetorical questions – these require no answer but are useful for grabbing attention and sowing the seeds of an idea: 'Here we are with bulging order books and plant that keeps breaking down. So where do we go from here? Well...'.

◆ Use summaries and introductions to reinforce your message: 'We've just seen how...what I'd now like to do is look at...'

Time how long each section takes (including the time it takes to talk through any slides or other visuals) by speaking, rather than reading, the presentation. This should be done at normal speaking speed (with pauses for dramatic effect as appropriate!). Note down the timings of key sections in your script and monitor them – they will help to stop you running out of time before the end – and also insert references to slides in your script (in large print or a different colour) to provide useful triggers.

Designing and using text slides

Some experts argue that although 'a picture is worth 1,000 words', text slides (where you are giving the audience words rather than visuals) are a waste of time.

Slides should never be a substitute for a good presentation, but can provide the means of bringing it to life with some punchy bullet points. You do need to follow the basic rules though.

Arguments against text slides

◆ They distract the audience's attention from what you are saying

◆ If the slide is just repeating the points you are making, why are you bothering with it?

◆ People listen at the same rate, but read at different rates.

Arguments for text slides

◆ They provide a useful support and reinforcement for a presentation, not least because they can capture your key points in summary

◆ If they are also given to your audience as handouts, they can be used for note taking during your presentation, and can be taken away and mulled over later.

Slides that succeed

Do keep them short and snappy (think advertising slogans, think T-shirts) with no more than five or six points per slide.

Do make them big enough to read. PowerPoint (the standard Microsoft Office presentation software) is formatted automatically; if you use Word for overhead transparencies (OHTs), aim for headings of around 18 point and text at 16 point, using bold and italic for emphasis.

Do check each slide to make sure it really is adding value; if not, bin it.

Do use a maximum of one slide per three minutes of formal presentation time.

Do use them to break up the texture of your presentation and to add impact and interest to it.

Do provide a low-tech back-up (for example a set of OHTs) in case of technical problems.

Do check that the technology is in place for displaying your slides (and the back-up if necessary) and that you know how to use it. Have a dry run in advance in the presentation venue if possible.

Don't be so distracted by the slides you take your eyes off the audience; you're presenting to people, not a screen. Print off a hard copy that you can keep in front of you.

Don't produce slides from tables of figures; no one will be able to read them, so be ruthlessly selective with numerical data.

Don't (unless you are very experienced) try lots of fancy stuff, with text and graphics whizzing in from all directions.

Don't produce slides of diagrams where text is set at different angles.

Don't overcrowd slides with more text and graphics than viewers can take in easily.

Using a video conference to make your presentation

If you are making your presentation to a remote audience using video-conferencing facilities you will probably modify your approach accordingly.

You may have access to an autocue system. If you do, find out what arrangements need to be made so that you can use it for your presentation. You will need to receive some guidance, training and practice in using it beforehand.

In video conferencing you are on camera. The equipment is usually low contrast and low resolution – which you should bear in mind when choosing what to wear. Because of the remote transmission there is often a gap between speaking and receiving – similar to long distance telephone calls, so you need to be more deliberate in the way you converse with people. The following tips for using video conferencing should help you to prepare to deliver your presentation remotely.

Video conferencing tips

◆ You should not have to worry about technical details – IT staff should set up the equipment, adjust cameras, sound and lighting. IT staff will also put away equipment etc. at the end of the conference. Check that they will be available for the time the conference is scheduled.

◆ If you are using PowerPoint slides during the presentation, make sure that all participants will be able to receive these. It may not be feasible to use these for the presentation.

◆ Circulate any documentation in advance, including any outline of the presentation and any PowerPoint images that you may want to deliver during the presentation.

◆ Brief the chairperson in advance about what to expect from your presentation – for example time, interaction with audience, outline of coverage.

◆ Wear pastel shades; avoid white and black; and use plain clothes without patterns.

◆ Arrive early for the conference so that you can settle in, get acquainted with the equipment, set-up and seating arrangements.

◆ Have a glass of water to hand during the conference.

◆ Begin the video conference with a sound check and camera check for all participants and make sure everyone is settled in before getting down to business.

- Most conferences are booked for a predetermined amount of time – make sure your presentation fits within the time allocated, allowing for two-way discussion.

- Sit up or stand so you can breathe and speak normally.

- Talk at a normal rate, pitch and tone. The microphone means you don't need to raise your voice.

- Make the presentation interactive: it is easy for a remote audience to switch off – watch out for signs of this among your audience such as not attending or fiddling – and pose questions or invite comment to keep the audience engaged.

- Allow for the slight delay in the transmission of video and audio when asking for questions or contributions from the audience. For example, do not rush the conversation and allow a contribution to end before initiating a new input.

- Do not interrupt another person as this will cut them off mid-sentence.

- Remain seated (or standing if this is the arrangement) so that the camera can stay trained on you. Have documents to hand so that you don't have to reach across a desk or go off-camera. Try to avoid white paper; you could use a coloured folder to hold your documents.

- If you feel a coughing fit coming on or need to discuss something off camera, use the mute button.

- Think about what action you want from participants, for example feedback on your ideas. You may want to invite them to think about an issue and circulate their ideas on it after the conference.

Source: *Adapted from University of Cambridge Computing Service* (1998)

◆ Recap

Identify the features of clear written communication

- Most documents are written for a purpose, for example to persuade or to inform. The first step in writing an effective document is to define what you want to achieve and what you want your readers to do.

- Information within the document should be presented so that it meets the needs and interests of your readers and is easily accessible. The most important information should be presented first.

Evaluate your writing style

- ◆ Effective business communication should:
    - – avoid sentences that are difficult to follow
    - – use simple, active language
    - – avoid double negatives
    - – use minimal jargon
    - – use bullet points/lists (when appropriate) to break up the text
    - – use appropriate punctuation, sentence structure and spelling.

Plan an effective presentation

- ◆ Be selective about what you include in a presentation. Focus on making a few really important points that will enable you to achieve your aim and will interest the audience.

- ◆ Shape these into a presentation structure that sets the scene, explains the issues and concludes by telling people what action is required next. Present keys points when the audience is most alert – at the start and end of the presentation.

Develop notes and visual aids to support your presentation

- ◆ Develop notes as a memory jogger for when you deliver your presentation but avoid writing a script. Small index cards that list the main points or key words are ideal.

- ◆ Use slides to reinforce your presentation and bring it to life. There are arguments for and against using text slides. If you do use them, follow the guidance in the 'Slides that succeed' checklist.

 More @

Walters, L. (2002) *Secrets of successful speakers*, McGraw-Hill
This is an excellent book for anyone wanting to develop their skills as a presenter.

Leigh, A. (1999) *Persuasive Reports and Proposals*, **Chartered Institute of Personnel and Development**
This handbook covers five crucial aspects which spell out the word 'PRIDE' – what you should feel about your documents if they are to win hearts and minds: Purpose, Readers, Image, Detail and Enhancers.

Strunk, W. and White, E. (1999) *The Elements of Style*, **Allyn & Bacon**
This classic text shows you how to be clear, concise and precise, and is itself written in a similar style.

Try the communications skills directory of **Mind Tools** at www.mindtools.com for advice on communicating in writing and on presentation skills.

Information systems

So far in this book we have focused on how you can improve your own management of information. But you are working within an infrastructure of organisational information and knowledge systems.

This theme explores the key issues in systems development and reviews how the Internet is transforming corporate communication systems. The massive growth in computer systems and the use of Web-based technology have attracted a corresponding rise in the number and variety of threats to security. With widespread desktop access to e-mail and the Internet, all managers – indeed all staff – need to be alert to the dangers of unauthorised access to an organisation's systems.

In this theme you will:

- Identify the key stages in the system development life cycle and your contribution towards it
- Identify the benefits of an corporate intranet
- Assess how well your organisation manages data security.

Key issues in systems development

It's a fair guess that many of your working hours are spent in front of a computer, using the information system in different ways: reading, inputting, organising and sending out data. Typically, there will be times when the system won't do what you want it to do, or you think, 'Why did they design it like this? Why can't I just go straight to... It's useless...' However, the way your system was designed probably originally depended (at least to some extent) on the way local users and managers described the jobs they wanted the system to perform. This legacy will have a crucial impact on the way you manage your own incoming and outgoing information and, by extension, the extent to which the organisation as a whole manages and makes accessible its information and knowledge resources.

At some point in your career you will be involved in providing input to a major system upgrade or replacement, even if you have not yet done so. Understanding how and why systems are developed, and the possible pitfalls, provides important lessons for managers involved in future systems development.

Systems model and life cycle

Computers have been with us for a long time, but their development has been surprisingly unpredictable. Up until the 1970s there were few attempts to produce a coherent view of computer operations. One of the first models was developed by Richard Anthony (Mason and Willcocks, 1994). This was actually a model of organisational behaviour, which put forward the view that there are three basic types of decisions made within organisations:

- ◆ **Strategic:** these involve setting overall goals and objectives and determining how to meet them
- ◆ **Control:** making sure that the organisation's functions are carried out efficiently and resources are used effectively
- ◆ **Operational:** relating to day-to-day operations, ensuring that tasks are done properly, in the right order, at the right time.

As a model, Anthony's pyramid (see Figure 4.1) has had a huge influence on management thinking – and will still be recognisable in your own organisation today. This hierarchical view of functions within the organisation was mirrored by the systems managers' approach, which was geared to the belief that the logical starting point for introducing computer applications was at the operational level, working upwards from there to the rarefied heights of supporting strategic business decisions.

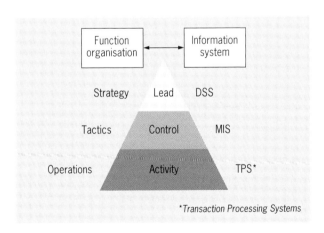

Figure 4.1 *Anthony's pyramid*   Source: *Mason and Willcocks* (1994)

From the late 1960s it was realised that systems development actually consisted of well-defined stages, and a 'life cycle' view of systems emerged that formed the basis of many different methodologies for systems development (Galliers et al. 1999). Even so, it took a long time to realise that the life cycle was not linear, with a neat start and end point, but needed to be viewed as a continuing process in order to:

- ◆ review and correct earlier errors and misconceptions

- ◆ revisit and retune the original specification in the light of changing requirements

- ◆ deal adequately with the problem of a growing number of systems involving increasing amounts of maintenance.

Figure 4.2 gives a graphical view of a system life cycle.

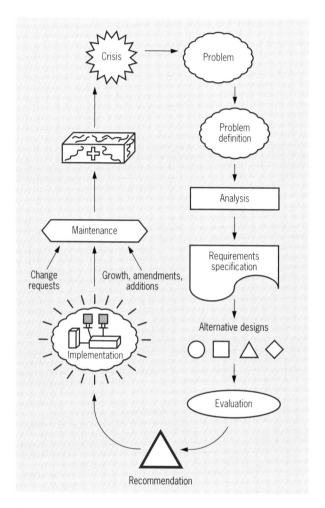

Figure 4.2 *The system life cycle*   Source: *Mason and Willcocks* (1994)

Your role in developing information systems

If you are not an IT manager, where do you fit into this process? You may not realise how important you are. Recent years have seen the growth of user involvement at every stage of systems development. As the impact of systems development has become visible and organisation wide, organisations have belatedly realised that it has a human dimension, and that ignoring this can wipe out all the advantages of your expensive new system.

Many organisations are now battling with the problem of so-called legacy systems. This is a system that was developed 20-odd years ago which was designed to solve the problems the organisation faced at that time. The trouble is that 20 years on, they are out of step with evolving business needs and can hold back organisations that want to apply a more up-to-date set of routines. They are now seen to be inflexible, expensive to maintain and even more expensive to replace. This has all lent urgency to the need for genuine user involvement in systems design, and few would dispute the necessity for this. But mistakes still happen. Lytle (1991) devised an information systems development disaster menu, shown in Figure 4.3, that still holds good. As you can see, it shows all the things you shouldn't do when developing computer systems. If you do, then you're heading for disaster.

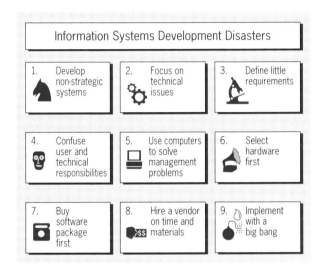

Figure 4.3 *An information systems disaster menu*   Source: *Lytle* (1991)

Let's turn the negatives from Figure 4.3 around and see what happens.

1 **Develop strategic systems.** What are the key *strategic information areas* for your business? These are your key business critical systems.

2 **Don't focus on technical issues.** Systems are not a matter of hardware and software; they are a matter of the *right* hardware and the *right* software, selected on the basis of user needs and organisational critical success factors.

3 **Take time to define requirements at 'big picture' and operational levels.** This is a key area of a manager's job. Welcome it as a real opportunity to examine quite critically what you are doing now. Do you still need to do it at all? Are there other, better ways of achieving your objectives? This will involve you in the following activities:

   ◆ Analysing all the business processes that you manage. For example, if you're an HR manager, this will include such areas as recruitment, appraisal and reward, workforce planning and job analysis and design. How do the functions that you manage fit into the wider organisational picture?

   ◆ Documenting the type of information you need to carry out your various tasks. Are you receiving everything you need, in the most efficient and timely way? Are you getting too much information, information you don't need at all or need less often?

♦ Drawing a picture of the data that flows in and out of your unit (don't forget to include informal data sources). What, and from where, are your data feeds? Who else receives the same information? What do you do with the information you receive? If you process it in some way, how is this done and what are the outputs? Who are they delivered to?

4 **Be clear about user and technical responsibilities.** Make sure that responsibilities are clearly defined at the outset, with staff allocated the roles that they are best qualified to do. That way you can build up co-operation and mutual respect, not mutual antagonism.

5 **Use management, not computers, to solve management problems.** Too often, problems that are actually related to poor management are conveniently blamed on 'the system'. Computers can do lots of things to improve your data management and information flow, but they can't resolve problems of organisational culture or personality clashes. Do what you can to get these issues resolved before your user specification gets underway.

6, 7 and 8 **Select hardware and software to fit the requirement, and be specific about any customisation required.** Adopt the motto 'focus on functionality'. Vendors are experts at showing off their systems to their best advantage, but will the system do what you want it to do? Can the software be customised, and will the vendor do this? Will they need to involve third-party suppliers? If customisation is required, get this specified in terms of activities and costs. Hiring on a time and materials basis is a recipe for a long drawn out, expensive and increasingly sour relationship.

Find out when the next version of the software is due. What do the licensing arrangements really mean in terms of multiple, real-time access? It is important to check out the vendor's financial stability as a standard procedure, and it may also be worth checking the business press to see whether the company (or its parent) is involved in merger discussions or is about to be swallowed by a giant competitor.

9 **Beware 'big bangs'.** It is rare now for a complete system to be developed in full before live operation, and for good reason. It takes time to develop a complete system, and while this is happening there will inevitably be evolution and change in user requirements. These need to be incorporated into the developing system and checked by the user to see if they work. It is much better to develop a prototype system that can be piloted (tested, reviewed and improved) and used to inform the final development.

Intranets and extranets

The idea of getting computers to communicate with each other, either on a one-to-one basis or via a network, has been around for a long time. Networks are of two main types, determined by the size of area that they cover:

◆ **Local area network (LAN)** which can link computers in a single room, one building or several buildings that are geographically close (for example on a university campus)

◆ **Wide area network (WAN)** which, as its name implies, can link computers that can be hundreds or even thousands of miles apart.

The widespread take-up of the Internet in recent years has transformed the way that networks are used, and added a whole new dimension (with new opportunities and new problems) to the way in which organisations communicate internally and externally.

An **intranet** is a network (LAN or WAN) that utilises Internet technology. However, unlike the Internet, access to an intranet is restricted to specific individuals, and the data it holds will be secured behind stringent data security systems or firewalls.

An **extranet** uses Internet technology to link together intranets in different locations. In contrast to intranet transactions, extranet transmissions take place over the Internet, and so are not secure. This necessitates strengthening the security of the connecting portions of the Internet. This can be done by creating 'tunnels' of secured data flows. The Internet with such tunnelling technology is known as a virtual private network (VPN) – see Figure 4.4.

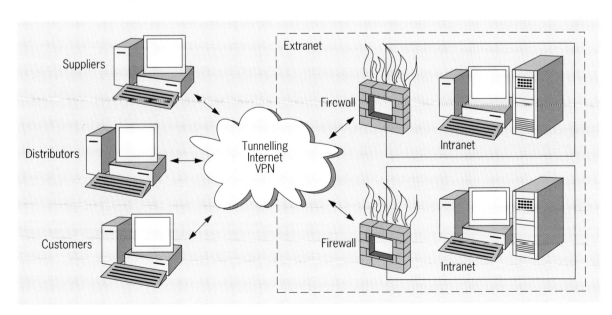

Figure 4.4 *Diagrammatic contrast of the Internet, intranet and extranet*

Source: *Turban et al.* (2000)

Both systems and departmental managers have been quick to seize the advantages of a corporate intranet:

> With businesses under significant pressure to empower employees and to better leverage internal information resources, intranets furnish a very effective communications platform – one that is timely and extensive. A basic intranet can be set up in days and can eventually act as an 'information hub' for the whole company... Intranets can provide the following features:
>
> ♦ easy navigation (internal home page provides links to information)
>
> ♦ ability to integrate a distributed computing strategy (localised web servers residing near the content author)
>
> ♦ rapid prototyping (can be measured in days or even hours in some cases)
>
> ♦ accessible via most computing platforms
>
> ♦ scaleable (start small, build as requirements dictate)
>
> ♦ extensible to many media types (video, audio, interactive applications)
>
> ♦ can be tied to 'legacy' information sources (databases, existing word processed documents, groupware [software designed for group communication and shared group use]).

Source: *Shim (2000)*

The potential business benefits of intranets are numerous (Fishenden, 1997):

♦ improved information flows between employees, customers and suppliers

♦ reduced geographical constraints: worldwide organisations can now communicate as a logical whole

♦ easy access to information through a common single interface

♦ better access to information = quicker and better decision making = reduced cost

♦ reduced cost of IT operations: Internet-derived technology is a cheap way of improving communication and data flows

♦ increasing an organisation's profile on an international scale: selected components of an intranet can be shared via a public interface on the Internet.

It can be used for a huge range of practical applications, from making corporate information available to all employees to providing specific information to a salesforce in the field or external stakeholder groups.

Albion Oil

Having secured a contract to assist with exploration and exploitation of natural resources in North Africa, Albion Oil needed a means of handling its rapidly growing information assets and communicating efficiently with all members of a project team scattered across Europe, North Africa and North America. A technical review of the existing infrastructure revealed a mix of Macs, PCs and UNIX systems. What to do? These are the steps they took:

♦ Produced a project initiation document defining key business objectives

♦ Restricted the scope of the project to users involved in the North African exploration

♦ Defined key deliverables, including the establishment of a user group

♦ Defined key success criteria – e.g. providing users with reliable and secure access to information and round-the-clock support and training

♦ Documentation, clarification of roles and responsibilities and mechanisms for addressing security, reliability, contingency and other issues were all established as necessary targets

♦ Clear targets were identified in terms of 'publishing' information (authoring, formats, ownership), locating information and Newsgroup 'netiquette'

♦ The project was controlled by a small tightly focused team

♦ Beginning with an online telephone directory of staff as a pilot, Albion moved to adopt the same approach to other project related data. The results have been a system that matched management and user requirements in which the technology was clearly focused and not just applied for its own sake.

Source: *Fishenden* (1997)

Activity 12
Identify useful content for your intranet

Objectives

Use this activity to:

♦ identify useful content for including on your intranet

♦ evaluate your organisation's intranet from a user's point of view.

Task

1 If you have an intranet, note down in the first column of the chart a selection of the content currently available on it (for example staff directory, training information, minutes of particular committees, product or project information).

2 Next note down whether you regard this information to be a useful facility or not, and why.

Content example	Useful or not?	Why?

3 If your organisation does not have an intranet, what would you like to have available on one? What benefits would you expect to accrue from this?

What content?	Expected benefit?

Feedback

What you learned from this activity will depend on whether your organisation has an intranet or not and, if it does, how well you rate it. If you have identified significant strengths, are there ways you can capitalise on them that you have not yet explored? If you have identified obvious weaknesses, why not put your ideas forward? If, on the other hand, you have considered what you would like to have available on an intranet, you may find it helpful to discuss the benefits you aim to achieve with a colleague or friend.

Data security

Security threats can present themselves in direct form, through hackers (and as far back as 1997 it was estimated that the Internet is hacked into every 20 seconds) and through indirect information systems penetration (Mitchell et al. 1999). These indirect threats occur in four major types:

- **Worms:** a worm is a program that, once established, can spread copies of itself throughout a network

- **Trojan horses:** these are also programs that appear to be carrying out a non-malicious activity which, when activated, reveal their true destructive intent

- **Logic bombs:** these are programs activated by a specific event, for example St Valentine's Day

- **Viruses:** like a medical virus, these 'infect' other programs.

A popular route in for these invaders is via e-mail – and they don't always come in as attachments. The header message is usually friendly and intriguing, encouraging the user to believe that it is a message from a friend or admirer.

The results of these attacks can range from the irritating and embarrassing to the devastating, and can include the destruction of data or its modification, interception or fabrication by unauthorised personnel.

The Melissa virus
Melissa was an e-mailed virus that emerged from nowhere to overwhelm commercial, government and military computer systems, leading the FBI to launch the biggest Internet manhunt ever.

Melissa affects Word 97 and Word 2000 documents. If launched, this virus will attempt to start Microsoft Outlook to send copies of the infected document to up to 50 people in Outlook's address book as an attachment.

The e-mail subject line reads:

Important message from [username]

While the message reads:

Here is that document you asked for ... don't show anyone else. ; –)

Source: *MelissaVirus.com* (www)

Viruses often spawn ever more dangerous variants. The 'I Love You' virus, which appeared in Spring 2000, had 50 variants by October that year.

The growth of e-commerce has seen a surge in opportunities for business fraud and other security issues.

KPMG survey

The management consultancy firm KPMG has produced some worrying findings from its 2001 *Global e-fr@ud Survey*:

♦ E-fraud is a growing problem for companies around the world.

♦ Although credit card numbers and personal information are of prime concern to customers, less than 35 per cent of companies surveyed have had security audits performed on their e-commerce systems.

♦ 50 per cent of businesses identified hackers and poor implementation of security policies as the greatest threats to their e-commerce systems. However, the company is at greater risk of being the victim of an internal security breach.

♦ 83 per cent of respondents feel that the public perceives the traditional 'bricks and mortar' business as more secure than e-commerce-based dot.coms.

Source: *Adapted from KPMG (2001)*

Methods of data security

There is a range of methods of varying complexity that organisations can use to protect themselves from unauthorised access. See Table 4.1.

Method	Description
Firewalls	The first line of defence from the outside. Acts as a security guard for the company's internal network, filtering all incoming traffic from the Internet. A good tool for networks connected to the Internet
User authentication	Verifies the identity of the user. Could also be used to restrict access to certain resources within the network. A requirement for any user accessing a corporate network
Data encryption	Scrambles the data before and during transmission. Use this method when data protection is important
Key management	Acts like a 'key' to access encrypted data. Maximum protection to protect data from unauthorised parties. Use in conjunction with data encryption
Digital certificate	Like a watermark on a bank cheque – this is an electronic ID card that establishes your credentials when doing business on the Web
Intrusion detection system (IDS)	Scans the network for abnormal activity and security breaches. A minimal requirement for any corporate network
Virus detection	Scans the network data for viruses, providing both prevention and cure if updated regularly. One of the best defences for data protection
Virtual private networks (VPN)	A secure private data network developed on a public data network like the Internet
Extranets	A secure private data network that uses a public data network like the Internet to extend a company's network to suppliers, vendors, partners, etc. A company can minimise its overheads by exchanging data through an extranet via electronic data interchange (EDI)

Table 4.1 *Methods of data security*　　　　　Source: *Hawkins et al.* (2000)

Data protection

Another aspect of information security is data protection. One of the effects of increasing globalisation of business activities and cross-border data transactions has been to raise awareness of the need to safeguard personal details which are held in either manual or electronic systems. Several basic principles of data protection have now been established and codified in law. For example, in the UK, anyone processing personal data must comply with the enforceable principles of good practice. These are that personal data (which includes facts and opinions, and information regarding the intentions of the holder of the data towards the individual) must be:

♦ fairly and lawfully processed

♦ processed for limited purposes (for example legitimate business purposes)

♦ adequate, relevant and not excessive

♦ accurate

♦ not kept longer than necessary

♦ processed in accordance with the data subject's rights

♦ secure

♦ not transferred to other countries without adequate protection.

71

Feedback

If you don't know about your organisation or department's security policies, you should find out. Do your IT colleagues know more? The key point is that security is everyone's responsibility. Managers can help to raise awareness of the risks and take action to make sure that the organisation and its departments have established contingency plans and have adopted good practice for the security of the information that they manage.

◆ Recap

Identify the key stages in the system development life cycle and your contribution towards it

- ◆ Systems pass through a series of stages during their development; problem definition and analysis, specification of requirements, design and evaluation of options, recommendation and implementation.

- ◆ Systems development should be seem as cyclical rather than linear. Maintenance is required on an ongoing basis to manage change requests, growth, amendments and additions.

- ◆ User involvement is critical at each stage of the life cycle if the system is to meet its purpose and be fit for use.

Identify the benefits of a corporate intranet

- ◆ Intranets utilise Internet technology and have become a very popular means of improving information flow and communication through an organisation.

- ◆ Access is restricted to authorised individuals and data is secured behind firewalls, making intranets a safe and cost-effective approach to networking.

- ◆ An effective intranet should have directories and search engines that make it easy for users to find and retrieve the information that they need. Achieving this level of user friendliness requires careful planning.

Assess how well your organisation manages data security

- ◆ Security threats present themselves directly from hackers and indirect threats of four major types: worms, viruses, Trojan horses and logic bombs.

- ◆ Data can be made more secure through the use of firewalls, user authentication, data encryption, key management, digital certificates, intrusion detection systems, virus detection software, virtual private networks and extranets.

♦ Organisations should minimise the risk to their data by designing and implementing data security and management policies.

▶▶ More @

Wilson, D. (2002) *Managing Information: IT for Business Processes*, **Butterworth-Heinemann**
This book provides a compelling rationale for organisations to use information management systems and for individuals to acquire the skills to manage and use the systems.

Cobham, D. and Curtis, G. (2004) *Business Information Systems: Analysis, Design and Practice*, **Financial Times Prentice Hall**
This book provides a comprehensive understanding of how information systems can aid the realisation of business objectives, covering topics from systems, design analysis and planning to data mining, business intelligence and knowledge management.

The online library **BetterManagement** at www.bettermanagement.com provides free articles and white papers on a whole range of management topics including information technology. Select LIBRARY.

You can access the Data Protection Act at **Her Majesty's Stationery Office** – www.hmso.gov.uk/acts/acts1998/19980029.htm

5 Knowledge management

Knowledge management has been hyped as a must-have business solution for a number of years now. However, quite what it is and how you are supposed to manage something so intangible is still a source of much confusion.

In this theme you will:

♦ Define knowledge management and its relationship to learning processes

♦ Identify the barriers to knowledge management

♦ Identify the critical success factors in knowledge management

♦ Mobilise knowledge management in your organisation.

How do you manage knowledge?

One of the problems in trying to define knowledge management is that it is sometimes difficult to see how it differs from information management. Swan et al. (2000) see the two as being very closely associated, with each interacting with the other. See Figure 5.1.

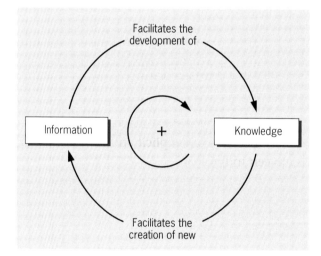

Figure 5.1 *The dynamic relationship between information and knowledge*

Source: *Swan et al.* (2000)

As explored in Theme 1, knowledge combines information, experience and insight into something that is unique to every individual. But what is knowledge management? Here are two definitions:

> Knowledge Management is the **explicit** and **systematic** management of **vital knowledge** and its associated **processes** of creating, gathering, organising, diffusion, use and exploitation. It requires turning personal knowledge into corporate knowledge that can be widely shared throughout an organisation and appropriately applied.

Source: *Skyrme* (www)

Or, put another way:

> Knowledge Management...has been described as 'knowing what you know, knowing what you don't know, learning what you need to know and sharing it.'

Source: *Newing* (2000)

It is worth being aware that different disciplines are concerned with recognising, valuing, capturing and measuring the knowledge and expertise within organisations, and adopt a range of terminology. Intellectual capital, for example, is a term that is often used alongside knowledge management. It has a broader definition than knowledge and comprises employees' talent and knowledge, customer loyalty, the value of brands, patents and copyrights and research. In this theme we focus on the concept of knowledge management given in the definitions from Skyrme and Newing above.

The concept of knowledge management grew in the early 1990s from a study of how Japanese companies create knowledge within the organisation, disseminate it and embody it in new products and services (Nonaka and Takeuchi, 1995). The Nonaka and Takeuchi model classified human knowledge into two kinds:

Explicit knowledge: this is formal, easily identifiable and general knowledge, the sort you find in mathematical expressions, or specifications and manuals. Because it is explicit and obvious, it can easily be transmitted between individuals.

Tacit knowledge: this is difficult to articulate, as it is personal, 'hidden' knowledge, embedded in an individual's experience and coloured by their personal beliefs and values.

These are the two basic building blocks of knowledge creation. The assumption is that knowledge is created through the dynamic interaction between explicit and tacit knowledge. For organisations to succeed, they need to find ways to make explicit and share the wealth of tacit knowledge that is locked up within individual employees' experience. Nonaka and Takeuchi saw the explicit/tacit relationship as a spiral process, in which interaction takes place repeatedly. Willard (1999) reworked and simplified their original spiral (see Figure 5.2), and sees the sequence in this way:

◆ Someone has a bright idea, and finds a way (sometimes easily, sometimes with great difficulty) of expressing that idea. This means that the idea moves from the *tacit* (personal knowledge and experience) to the *explicit* – expressed in a way that everyone can understand.

◆ The person who had the idea combines this with other known elements to form some kind of context (so we have *explicit* added to *explicit*).

◆ This is then communicated to colleagues, who begin to 'get the picture' and start to think about it on the basis of their own knowledge (so the *explicit* idea moves to *tacit* reflection and analysis).

◆ Through discussion the idea grows and develops, and colleagues all contribute to the implicit understanding that builds up (adding *tacit* to *tacit*).

◆ New ways are found to express the idea, more people are informed and the idea is increasingly combined to present a bigger idea (and so on).

◆ The new understanding is now institutionalised – turned into a working procedure or implemented as a working practice or rule.

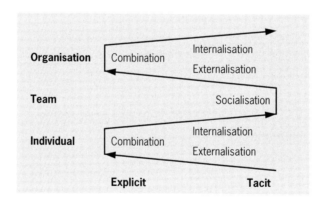

Figure 5.2 *The knowledge spiral*   Source: *Willard* (1999)

Much of the literature about knowledge management relates to the technology: the systems for sharing and exploiting the newly explicit knowledge. However, knowledge management is actually about people and their interaction, rather than technology – though technology is a powerful enabler.

Knowledge management and learning

An important aspect of knowledge management is the way people (and organisations) learn and how they approach problem solving. This is a good point to revisit Argyris and Schön's theories-in-use (the private, self-generated theories that govern our behaviour).

Argyris and Schön (1974) built a model of the processes involved in the theory in practice (see Figure 5.3) that has three elements:

◆ **Governing variables (or values):** there are likely to be a number of these and any action taken is likely to impact on them.

◆ **Action strategies:** what people do to keep their governing values within an acceptable range.

◆ **Consequences:** what happens as the result of an action. Consequences can be intended or unintended.

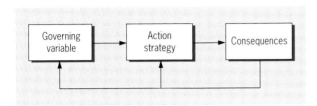

Figure 5.3 *Theory-in-use model*   Source: *Smith* (2001)

Where the consequences of your action strategy are in accord with your governing values, the theory-in-use is confirmed. But what happens if the consequences work against your governing values?

Argyris and Schön suggest that there are two responses to this mismatch, which they describe as **single-loop learning** and **double-loop learning**. When something goes wrong, a common response is to look for another strategy that will work better, but still within the framework of existing governing variables or values – the plans, goals or rules of behaviour that we are familiar with. This is single-loop learning. A more radical approach is to examine critically the governing variables or values themselves, to test how valid they still are. This in turn can lead to a change in the whole framework in which the action strategies and consequences are developed – a double-loop (see Figure 5.4).

How does this translate into organisational learning and behaviour? Looked at in organisational terms, error and correction in a single-loop learning environment will work within the organisation's existing policies and objectives, but otherwise carry on with these unchanged. Double-loop learning will occur when errors are corrected in ways that involve the modification of the organisation's underlying norms, policies and objectives. Argyris and Schön argue that double-loop learning must be maximised if organisations are to make informed decisions in rapidly changing contexts. It is an approach which accords very well with the underlying values of knowledge management.

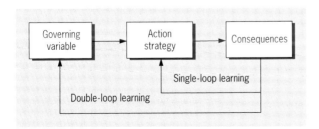

Figure 5.4 *Double-loop learning*   Source: *Smith* (2001)

If you're still wondering what use knowledge management is, take a minute to think about the following case study.

> **Case study**
> A specific example of this corporate amnesia can be found at Ford, where new car developers wanted to replicate the success of the original Taurus design team. But no one remembered, or had recorded, what was so special about that effort... The assumption that technology can replace human knowledge or create its equivalent has proven false time and again.
>
> Source: *Davenport and Prusak* (1998)

Business benefits of knowledge management

Several business benefits have been identified as accruing from knowledge management (Newing, 2000):

◆ identifying new markets from high-level intelligence gathering and pooling of knowledge by experts

◆ more responsiveness to market needs by harnessing external knowledge

◆ using customer knowledge to improve existing products and create innovative new ones

◆ faster time to market

◆ better quality products

◆ reusing knowledge gained in other parts of the world for other customers with similar problems

◆ continuous learning and development of best practice

◆ reducing costs associated with finding and reinventing knowledge by quickly retrieving explicit knowledge already stored

◆ improving customer service by applying knowledge at the point of first interaction with the customer

◆ reduction of risk by using wider expertise.

> Of all the initiatives we've undertaken at Chevron during the 1990s, few have been as important or as rewarding as our efforts to build a learning organization by sharing and managing knowledge throughout our company.
>
> Source: *Derr* (www)

Accepting the theory, and acknowledging the benefits, is a good starting point. But there can be considerable challenges and problems, which we will look at next.

Challenges and critical success factors

As a concept, knowledge management can involve some fundamental rethinking about the value of individual knowledge, and how the retention or sharing of knowledge by individuals is perceived and rewarded by the employing organisation. The argument runs: 'If knowledge is power, why should I diminish (or eliminate) my power base by sharing it?' This is one of many challenges that management faces in introducing knowledge management. Here we examine some of the key issues and the critical success factors.

Barriers to knowledge management

Even if your organisation has taken on board the message that using your corporate knowledge more intelligently can be a vital component in competing in the marketplace, it may well face a number of basic problems before it can get underway (Bonaventura, 1997). There may be, for example:

- no model for knowledge creation and dissemination within the organisation: you've never done it before so where do you start?
- no processes or systems focused on supporting those activities – they weren't part of the original systems specification so where do they fit in now?
- no systems able to measure or evaluate how well you are creating and disseminating knowledge
- no means of evaluating the effectiveness of the knowledge creation and dissemination activities that you are carrying out.

Von Krogh et al. (2000) believe that managers ought to be supporting knowledge rather than trying to manage it, as it is basically unmanageable and not amenable to traditional management techniques. Individual staff may be reluctant to accept new lessons, insights and ideas, and many organisations can be quite challenging places for people learning to overcome the barriers of sharing knowledge with others. Individual barriers can include the following:

- People approach new experiences on the basis of their experience and beliefs about the world. There will be some situations which are so new and different that they will not have developed a response to them, and will find them too challenging.

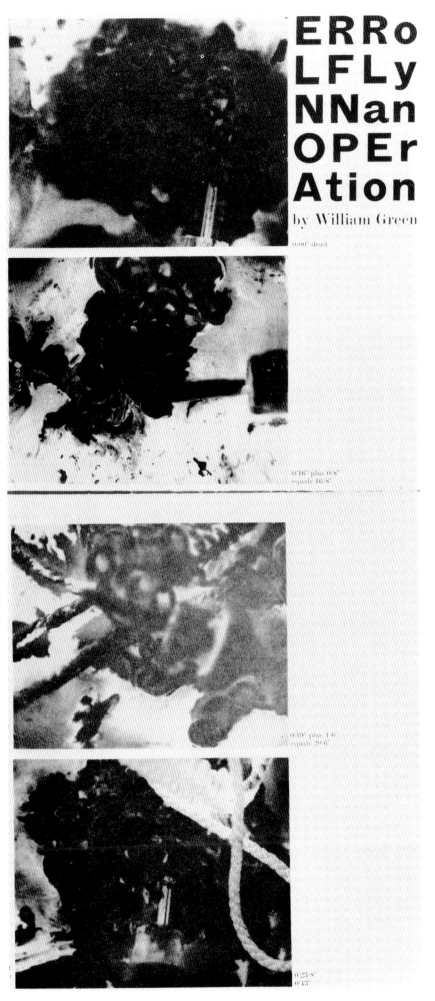

ERRo LFLy NNan OPEr Ation

by William Green

Errol Flynn the star was dead ... but Green appropriated his name for his December 1959 show at the New Vision Centre. Denis Bowen, Director of the gallery, told the *Daily Herald*, 'Flynn's name is good publicity ... it will bring the people in'.

William Green,
ERROLFLyNNanOPErAtion,
1959 (ARK magazine)

Denis Bowen,
Photograph of William Green,
1959

William Green,
Elvis, 1958–59
Photostatic print, 20 x 15 cm
Roddy Maude-Roxby

Linda McCartney,
Pete Townshend,
Photograph, 1967

A brooding Viennese romanticism hovered over his black monochromes.

The sub-cultural and media notoriety of the 'Beat Rebel' was eulogised by Green's RCA contemporaries such as Michael Chalk; but an extraordinary productivity and invention was present in his art. Green's *Elvis* (1958–59) took Surrealist protocols of treating photography into the epoch of pop-culture with a raw, disfiguring edge. Elvis, Napoleon and Errol Flynn, Romantic heroes all, are dissected in his paintings and treated photographs, to uncover the hearts of darkness embedded deep in their fame. Green's epic painting (with its echoes of Mathieu's cult of martial figures), *Napoleon's Chest at Moscow* (1957), which Alloway had included in his 'Dimensions' exhibition in December 1957, revolved around the sorrow and disappointment apocryphally written onto Napoleon's body (a blackened, broken heart). *ERROLFLyNNanOPErAtion* (1959) mimicked the discourses of medicine as allegories for the act of painting. The swirling, dark organics of blood and X-ray shadows ornamentalised body fluids into patterns of painterly flow. They were documents of a fictional performance piece, where Action painting punned on surgery; as Roddy Maude-Roxby wrote of the treated photographs by Green, '*ERROLFLyNNanOPErAtion* was performed with a series of photostats'.[16] As Mathieu had shown in his 'performance' of his painting *The Battle of Hastings* at the ICA in 1956, Action painting had become involved with duration and fantastic grand fictions. The timetable of the performed painting/action became a key document – Green drew one up for his *Portrait of Michael Davies* (1958) – and the notion of the art work as notated event in time underlay John Latham's first theorising of the 'event-structure' in 1959. Gustav Metzger, the founder of Auto-Destructive Art, also found Green's eight foot bitumen monochromes, 'a great influence'.[17] Both Metzger and Green in their turn influenced Pete Townshend, later of The Who, at Harrow and Ealing Schools of Art. Their destructive activities, their 'generous violence', appeared as a portent to Townshend; by 1966 he had incorporated 'auto-destruction' in The Who's stage act.

Errol Flynn the star was dead, but Green appropriated his name for his December 1959 show at the New Vision Centre. Denis Bowen, Director of the gallery, told the *Daily Herald*, 'Flynn's name is good publicity ... it will bring the people in'.[18] A couple of months later Alloway exalted Green's action as a paradigm of the freed new abstraction in all its allusiveness and ambiguity: it was ' "Pop as Polemic and Affiliation" ... the title declares the artist's affiliation: what else he is interested in besides art ... the spectator's freedom and projective capacity is not interfered with. The words are a guide not to reaching the picture but to the kind of man who made it ...'[19] In other words, the painting's identity devolved upon its creator who roamed the archives of low and high culture. Alloway, with Richard Smith, was insisting upon anti-formalist destinations for abstraction, a voluntaristic inclusion of free-floating 'content', that would propel it towards the 'hot' environments of 'Place' and 'Situation', paving the way, as the decade began, to a redefining of abstract art.

Denis Postle,
Photograph of Eduardo Paolozzi's **The Frog,**
1959

Tony Messenger,
Photograph of
Michael Davies,
William Green
and Michael Chalk
standing by Green's
Hudson Terraplane,
June 1958

Michael Chalk had imagined Green, 'rather than museum bound ... around the breaker's yards'

Gwyther Irwin,
1959

If Green's cutting into the bodies of the famous was gratuitous and colluded with media systems of publicity and promotion, Eduardo Paolozzi's founding gestures of Brutalism had been directed along other lines. Nevertheless the tactic of exposing beneath an epidermis was employed by him as well. The skin in question was metallic but it carried an organic metaphor, rearranging the guts of technology by collage principles, as with the sculpture at his Hanover Gallery exhibition in 1958. Paolozzi's continued resistance to formalism positioned him in opposition to the dominant St. Martin's sculpture through the Sixties. This resistance depended upon his use of collective and popular memory – of industrial fantasies – and it resulted in a dense layering of content. His interleaved imagery raucously paralleled R.B. Kitaj's, and there came a moment in the early Sixties when he collaborated with Kitaj on collages. His love of profane modernity stood altogether at odds with the Greenbergian and phenomenological 'modernist reduction'. As the Fifties closed, the collage and assemblage aspects of the 'Junk aesthetic' had become an international style. Michael Chalk had imagined Green, 'rather than museum bound he'll be around the breaker's yards'.[20] But it was not to purify such battered forms – as Caro was to do from the spring of 1960 – that Paolozzi and other 'Junk' artists laboured. On the contrary, where St. Martin's would react against such cues of organic entropy – surface patina, distress and oxidisation – as metaphors for the body, 'Junk' assemblagists such as Gwyther Irwin and Stuart Brisley regarded these qualities as essential virtues.

As with Green, the illicit, violent and socially transgressive was bound up in the process of image scavenging by Irwin and Brisley. As a student in Munich in 1959–60, Brisley found that 'the theft of materials was an essential ingredient'.[21] Again, as in Green's case, a metaphoric human anatomy was disclosed by Brisley in the scavenged objects: 'akin to the experiencing of one's own body which was the representation found in the matter, the material of the work'.[22] This was a vital step on the way to his own performance works that began around 1966. At the Alloway curated '3 Collagists' exhibition at the ICA in November 1958, Irwin referred to encounters with the Metropolitan Police during his theft of posters which he shredded into large scale montages.[23] Police knowledge of William Green's parallel activities, through his TV appearances, generally made them lenient on Irwin when he claimed kinship with Green and his methods.[24] But the unstable, catastrophic character of this art was not lost on Alloway when he compared the internal rhythms in Irwin's wall-like, gigantic, twelve-feet by sixteen-feet collage, *Thornton Maximus* (1960) to the 'undulations of collapsing brickwork'.[25] Denny, too, produced lettered paintings that have a relation to Irwin's torn printed word collages such as *Letter Rain* (1958). Through 1957–8, Denny stencilled brief words – terse Beat-culture and Rock 'n' Roll performatives and imperatives such as GO GO GO and MAN MAN, for his Molton Gallery exhibition in 1958. If Green had tried, like a Sadian surgeon, to penetrate beneath the skin of personified media images, Denny dismantled a linguistic body of 'good English' (and by implication the codes of gentility and social ranking and deference) with these works. Roger

As with Green, the illicit, violent and socially transgressive was bound up in the process of image scavenging by Irwin and Brisley ... 'the theft of materials was an essential ingredient'.

Gwyther Irwin,
Letter Rain, 1959
Collage on board,
183 x 91 cm
Artist's collection

Previous page:
Robyn Denny,
Wideaway, 1957–8
Oil on board, 152 x 244 cm
Artist's collection

Gillian Ayres
in her garden,
1959

Coleman likened them to the BBC Radio *Goon Show* in their capacity for manic anarchic disruption, 'sounds that have no message and no logic, except the logic of inspired pointlessness'.[26] The devices of dissent were being sharpened.

Action-based art in London at the end of the Fifties cannot, however, be reduced to one single pattern of raw and romantic resistance to social norms of gentility. The painting of Gillian Ayres, unlike that of Smith, Denny and Green, did not implicate itself in the cultural content of the 'information society' or anxieties around the body, but suggested instead a pure lyricism of colour that veered towards affirmative images of plenitude rather than horror. Promoting the new art of Denny, Smith, Green and Ayres in Rome, in 1958, Alloway wrote: 'Gesture, the visible sign of the artist's action in making his work of art, has been adopted as a method by a new generation. The tense poise of Smith, the spilled cornucopia of Ayres, the brutal skids and slashes of Green, for example, all depend on the artists' close sensual relation with their paint'.[27] In 1957 Ayres completed the first large public scale Action-style decoration in London, in collaboration with the architect Michael Greenwood. This was for the dinner hall of South Hampstead High School for Girls, using modules of eighty-inch blockboard of various widths between three to eleven feet in length: 'They are not framed', Alloway wrote, 'but slotted into one wall with doors and service counter interrupting the explosive showers of sensual paint. This is the first use of *tachisme* to decorate a British building'.[28] Ridiculed by the workmen who were busy on the project – who felt she was 'mucking up'[29] – Ayres mixed liberal amounts of turps into her oil paints to maintain a liquid flow; her understanding of Pollock's Action technique being based primarily on a viewing of the Hans Namuth film of Pollock painting (which may also have been the inspiration for Ken Russell's film of William Green, *Painting an Action Painting*).

Possibly an issue of gender entered into readings and interpretations of Ayres' gestural paintings from this moment. This came about through a concentration upon the painterly signifiers of fecundity; what Alloway, in the catalogue to Ayres' exhibition at the Molton Gallery in October 1960, called 'luxuriant'.[30] Two years later she wrote an experimental text which tried to account for the opening up – for her – of areas of subjectivity, while painting in what might now be thought of as a form of *écriture feminine*.[31] This interior flow of consciousness recounted her somatic experiences which were intimate with the act of painting, as if the painting and her body were speaking of the event: 'A shape – a relationship – a body – oddness – shock – mood – cramped ...'[32] With acute observation she defined a phenomenon in painting that was to form much of Sixties art sensibility. It had been evident in John Latham and then in Bernard Cohen's use of sprays from 1954 and 1961 respectively, and it was evident, too, in the paintings of Kenneth Noland which became like talismans of a new art for Anthony Caro and other sculptors such as Tim Scott. Ayres wrote of 'Painting's own nature – a mark making its own image in its own space.'[33] This forward grasp on the formative creed of self-reflexive art is qualified in Ayres by a lyricism and permissiveness to read her paintings of 1957–60 in associative ways: Alloway, in 1960, presented her as another exemplar of

Gillian Ayres,
Cumuli, 1959
Oil on hardboard, 304 x 320 cm
Artist's collection

Ayres wrote of 'Painting's own nature – a mark making its own image in its own space'.

how 'objectless colour, in mobile and dramatic configurations ... tends to mingle painterly and referential qualities ...'[34] For her part, the associative references were an evocation of 'a feeling of flowers, minerals, feathers or whatever it may be to different viewers'.[35] Her statement takes on a new light when seen in the context of photographs of her in the summer of 1959. She is in her back garden at Barnes, holding large paintings that seem to extend into the foliage of the trees around her and the clouds above, just as with the painting for the 'Situation' exhibition of the following year, which was called *Cumuli*, clouds.

John Minton's last 'Sketch Club'
Speech given at the Royal College of Art, 1956 [from a transcript made on the occasion by Anne Martin]

'(...) So you order your sack of cement **1** and put on the Nescafe and begin to paint your board on the floor – not on the easel! That's original, no one else does that. **2** Then you jump on it, off centre, that's to show you're sensitive. Then you paint a few dozen, pay someone to write a preface to the catalogue, number them, give them names, (...)
[You could call it anything, you could call it, *Eden Come Home* **3** or] (...) *Vistavision Film Company,* **4** you could build it for 2 million only – the price of an atom bomb or two films (...) You sit in the espresso bar with your portfolio and wonder what you're doing **5** (...) Keep away, keep away, an atom bomb falls, [but] you're all right, you're doing your abstract and problems are crowding round you like the furniture, till 'put out the light' when you can't bear it no longer. Is it to do with being blinded? **6**

(...)
I'm going to stay in to do my abstract today, Arthur, painting by the yard. 'Put the painting on the floor John and hang this piece of floor.' **7**

1 *Minton's embittered and satirical speech about current modes of painting was a scatter-gun attack on art brut, Action and informal methods. The 'sack of cement' he mentions at this point referred to Dubuffet's 'pates and Tapis' techniques.*

2 *Knowledge of Pollock's means of painting on the ground had been widely disseminated by the short film of him painting. William Green is likely to have been the other butt of Minton's ironic humour here.*

3 *It was at this point that Minton, looking at Robyn Denny's large, burned abstract painting, sarcastically suggested that he arbitrarily take the headline from a tabloid newspaper on the floor which called for the ailing Prime Minister's recall.*

4 *This seems to refer to Richard Smith, Denny's partner in cultural crime, in Minton's eyes. Smith had begun to theorise, with Roger Coleman and Lawrence Alloway, the new wide-screen cinema of Cinemascope and Vistavision as inaugurating a new experience of pictorial space.*

5 *Minton's caricature view of the beatnik lifestyle of 'The Angry Young Man'.*

6 *Minton's talk took place only a few weeks after Soviet Russia had threatened to bombard London and Paris with nuclear-tipped ballistic missiles. The furniture that crowds round in Minton's fantasy is his black comedy version of Civil Defence advice to prepare a 'Safe Room' in the period before atomic war, with furniture heaped up to protect shelterers in the room's centre.*

7 *His conclusion took the form of an imaginary exchange with one of the Painting School assistants, Arthur. The final sentence seems to be Arthur giving some common-sensical advice to Minton to simply hang the piece of floor as a painting In its own right.*

Platform
Roddy Maude Roxby, Robyn Denny and Dick Smith, An Open Letter to John Minton, *Newsheet,* December 1956

Platform
People are talking about Mr Minton's criticism of the Sketch Club, delighted that he could feel so committed as to be devastating. So often we see a harpoon poised and then, hesitation, the thought 'Dear Old Moby Dick' and the whale of our lethargy is allowed to slip on. Mr Minton was prepared to throw himself with his harpoon. Afterwards many were asking what R. Denny and R. Smith, the two most attacked, had thought of it all. They were as pleased as the rest to have a criticism given with such integrity but we wanted them to defend their view point, the cause of the bombardment.

An open letter to John Minton
or a stiffie on whose easel

Dear John Minton,
While welcoming your criticism of our paintings, we want to make clear our attitude towards painting, and our present situation (or predicament as you would prefer) which we feel that you have misunderstood because of what you described as your increasing sense of isolation from our generation. We are not disillusioned with the world. There is not a God that failed us. To your generation the thirties meant the Spanish Civil War; to us it means Astaire and Rogers. For you 'today' suggests angry young men, rebels without causes; we believe in the dynamism of the times, where painting being inseparable from the whole is an exciting problem linked now more than ever with the whole world problem of communication and makes its essential contribution to the total which is knowledge. Our culture heroes are not Colin Wilson and John Osborne, rather Floyd Patterson and Col. Peter Everest are more likely candidates for the title. Painting is an activity you can accomplish alone, but being alone does not of itself create an ivory tower Our tower is not more cut off from the world than those in Manhattan.
Yours sincerely
ROBYN DENNY
DICK SMITH

Sic, Sic, Sic
Lawrence Alloway, *Arts News and Review,* January, 1959

(...)
The New American Painting was unusual in that the exhibition was simultaneously an important memorial show and a display of the avant-garde. Usually exhibitions with the support of Governments are well past controversy (except behind the scenes): their public reception is placidly assured.
(...)
The reaction of the British press on the levels of protocol and cerebration, makes a strange record.

The Daily Telegraph made a triple assault on the show (presumably co-ordinated but, if not, symptomatic of anti-American attitudes). First Peterborough sneered at the catalogue ('portentous'); next the art critic, Terence Mullaly, who, for once, verged on the outspoken, wrote: 'it is the critic's duty to say that the pretensions (sic) of many of these artists seem as shallow as the extent of their influence is disgusting'. Curiously he projected an aura of disgust onto the exhibition, (sure to disgust *Telegraph* readers, I imagine), with his claim that the paintings 'represent a *surrender* to the *voluptuous*' (my italics). Next, a column called 'Way of the World' included this outburst: 'Acres of canvas, covered with blobs, stripes, scrawls, smears, runnels, drips, filth'; 'Utterly degenerate'; 'muck, lucrative muck'. These 'fraudulent absurdities' made the writer regret that 'Hitler died too soon'. To get the full weight of that it is worth remembering that some of the American artists at the Tate are Jews. Readers may like to know that the writers of this column describe themselves as 'Tory humourists' (sic). Their identities (under the byline 'Peter Simple'): Colin Welch and Peter Wharton. Remember these names.
According to David Carritt in the *Evening Standard* the American painters 'like *certain high-brow jazzmen* .... have evolved a new type of background art, perfect for *penthouse parties*, and often rising to the very highest level of triviality' (my italics again). Mr Carrit should be careful outside the Country House sleuthing circuit:

those jazzmen and those penthouses typify different periods, different tastes. A nasty failure in the connoisseurship of pop: you can't write smartly in this style with moth-ball information. Mr Carritt also collected some names from the catalogue for sneers at these painters, 'freed by Kierkegaard, Len (sic) Buddhism, and art collector Peggy Guggenheim'.

(...)

To send everybody home laughing I have kept the Home Service variety show *The Critics* (sic) till last. Harold Hobson quoted a lady-friend who had said of Newman's *Adam:* 'to me this is a symbolic representation of the unhappy and sorry condition of the human race' (including Eve?) If these paintings are done intuitively, he wanted to know, was a 'purely intuitive reaction' like that valid? Nobody told him the answer, so I will: it's no.

(...)

What can we conclude from this unhappy record of our critics' failure to either enjoy sympathetically or to criticise responsibly American Art? They failed to fill adequately either of the main roles open to them: they were neither opinion leaders, taste makers, nor interpreters, witnesses. The majority revealed a total inability to interpret documentary evidence attached to works of art because most of them lack any art historical training, but it was not made up by the amateur's traditional attribute of sensitivity.

(...)

William Green
Michael Chalk, Text for New Vision Centre Catalogue, July 1958

I'm no psychiatrist but knowing William gets you complex conscious and while you're worrying, he's hard at it going like hell. Unpredictable, he often catches the more prosaic off guard with alarming bursts of enthusiasm and likely as not goes berserk on formal occasions.

Rather than museum bound he'll be around the breaker's yard. Fingering the surface rust on Buick chrome. Slanging with the greasemonkeys or boost charging his day with road kicks, twenty four hour benders and then suddenly it's an extensive work period.

Owning a whalelike Hudson Terraplane resulted in a parked identity until the recent change to an even more sinister Packard straight eight. With an unquelled streak he handles a drag with unhesitant force, crams in that extra double feature and still has time for long studio workouts. Events on the floorlevel boards are handled with the same tense certainty: fresh pools of bitumen seal off the crust of past frenzies until the painting has stretched itself out to its full extent. Without a drawing-painting setup, that is with no idea start, the development of each work, while undergoing several free active bouts eventually jells into a state of formal stability. In *Owens and McGil* the medium was literally beaten into shape, with none of that brush jazz. They reflect the glossy sheen and accessories of a $17,500 drive away.

Clear of any objective associations some paintings however become curiously linked with, as the painter puts it, 'factual elements' that mentally persist while he works. *Bobby Greenlease – Carl Hall – Bonny Heddy* for instance, normally hangs in my studio remindful of that popular murder.

You don't have to study these exhibits to sense here blows a crazyheaded talent; it may be a one man with an answer – our beat painter who became a worldwide scoop.

Statement
Gillian Ayres,1962

A mark with a brush, on a chosen area of canvas – primed with G.P. Undercoat – dry or wet with turps – with colour – paint consistency – size – weight (tone).

A shape – a relationship – a body – oddness – shock – mood – cramped – isolated – acid – sweet – encroaching – pivoting – fading – bruised.

Painting's own nature – a mark making its own image in its own space – the canvas viewed as a whole image and space – an essence – perhaps like a space a sailor of Magellan's would have felt when the world was flat and he had sailed off the edge.

It's 'rubbish' with a high price tag.....Yet another way to 'paint'.

Keystone Press extended caption to picture story on Gwyther Irwin's 'Junk' Collages, early 1959.

Painting, or we should say, producing modern art, in a uniquely modern way is 28 year old ex-Gordonstoun scholar Gwyther Irwin.

Part of his skill lies in his ability to dodge police as he roams near his studios in Bushey, Herts., picking up old posters and general rubbish.

For all these things are constructed into surrealistic colourful artworks that are bringing in prices STARTING at £1,000.

He calls them collages and is presently working on a massive 20ft long epic that will incorporate more than 50 pounds of rubbish.

Mr Irwin has his art in practically every gallery in the world including the famed Guggenheim's Gallery in New York.

[The] Cornish born artist has sold 40 collages since he started this form of art in 1957 and he insists that he isn't interested in the fronts of the posters..... just the backs. 'The older they are the better', he says, 'and when the strips are pasted on canvas, they produce a wonderful translucent effect. I find the best ones in the East End and the police are always busy picking me up for acting suspiciously ... but they always have a good laugh when they find out my reasons.'

Besides finishing the mammoth collage he is working on one made entirely of string and soon after spending most of his life in art he is to start his first oil painting.

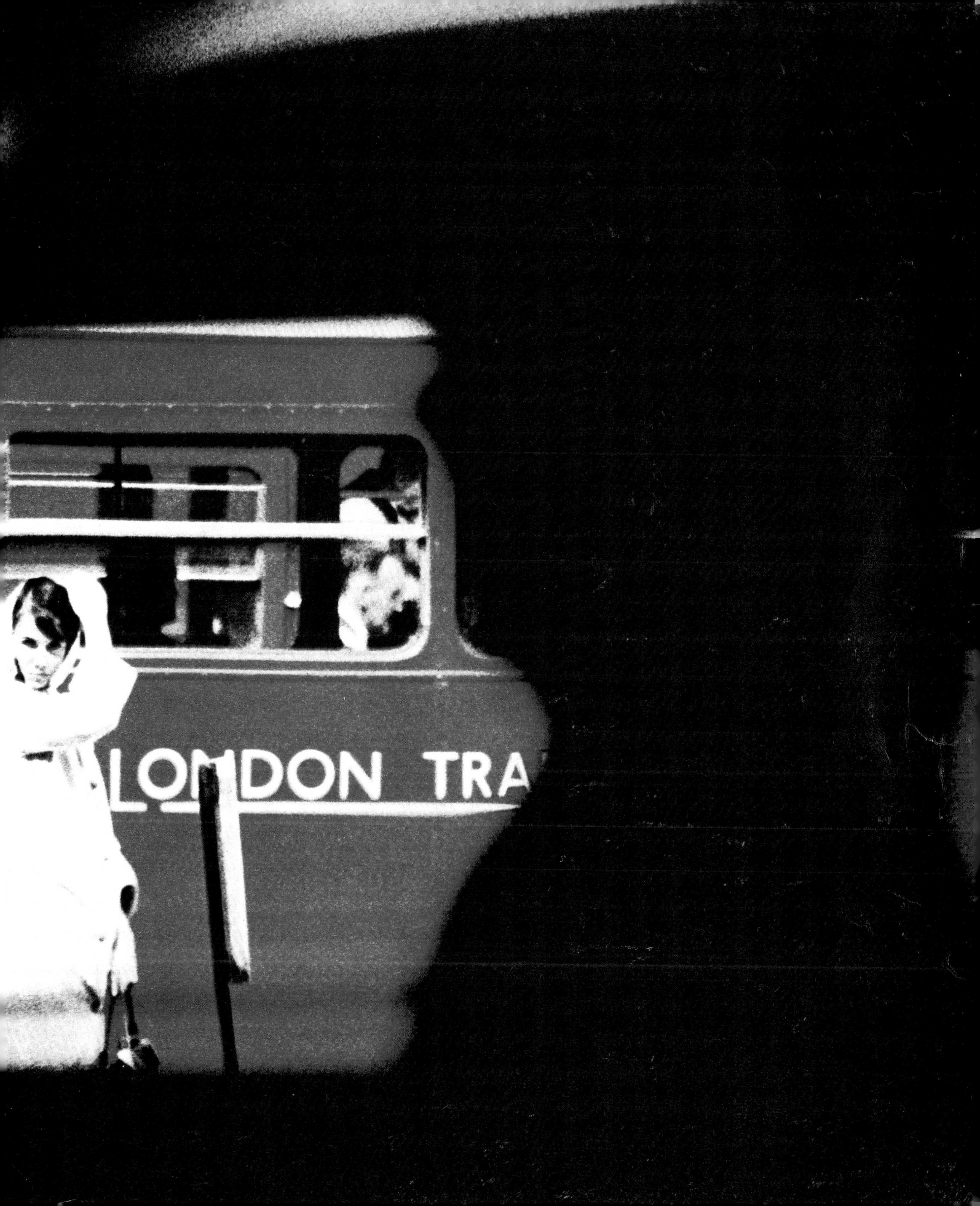
LONDON TRA

... metropolitan and urban culture seemed to be in passage, moving towards a city experienced as a speedy patterning of abrupt signs ...

Jock Kinneir and Margaret Calvert,
Cover of **HMSO Report on Traffic Signs**, 1963

Opposite: Archigram,
Logo for **Living City exhibition**, ICA, 1963

a rediscovered heroism of modern life – in Baudelaire's concept of mid-nineteenth century Paris. As a prelude to the epic of 'Swinging London' it was more than apt that on one of their first publicity sessions in London, the Beatles were photographed by Anthony Gales in front of the mural at Austin Reed.

As a first stage, between 1960 and 1963, London was imagined in the welter of the process – the colour and blur – of transformation. In Sidney J. Furie's widescreen and Technicolor direction of *The Young Ones* (1961) Cliff Richard's father is a property developer specialising in office blocks. This cinematic London is sited between small artisanal shops, streets, youth clubs and the new high-rise buildings, continually interrupted by red blurred buses, like the saturated red Bus canvases of Allen Jones from 1962. The cover of Colin MacInnes' *City of any Dream* (1962) shows a cloud of granular red which resolves into a bus. This photograph and others in the book by Erwin Feiger anticipated the hallucinated grain of the insubstantial metropolitan fragments in Michelangelo Antonioni's film, *Blow-Up* (1967). (In *Blow-Up* this topic, beside being attached to the theme of the delusions of photography, found itself figured by Antonioni through the display of Ian Stephenson's diffused, granular-surfaced paintings in the artist's studio next to the photographer's.)

Advertising and marketing were prompt at using the allusive imagery of Pop, 'feeding back' into a hardening myth of London as a witty, polychrome city. This was evident in Alan Fletcher's promotional work for Pirelli, which also capitalised on the flat, touristic, emblematic side of the London Routemaster bus. The road systems of the West End of London began to be remade into fast moving routes from 1961, most obviously with the remaking of Park Lane and the building of the Hammersmith flyover. The typographer and graphic designer Herbert Spencer photographed these sites for his article 'Mile a Minute Typography' published at the end of the year,[6] as assemblages of improvised signs, with urban mega-structures rising about them. He recorded the large arrows painted onto corrugated iron sheets on Park Lane's central reservation interrupted by the passing speed smears of Renault Dauphin minicabs carrying advertising for Cyril Lord carpets. The Renault Dauphin was, according to Op artist Peter Sedgley, who worked as a minicab driver at this time, the preferred vehicle of 'artists, layabouts and criminals'.[7] In the same summer of 1961 these arrow signs also drew the attention of Robert Freeman, a young Cambridge graduate friend of Alloway and temporary ICA organiser, who was making his way in London as a photographer. Later in 1963, he presented an account of London for *Living Arts* magazine, which showed it in a very different manner to Tony Armstrong-Jones' 1958 version of atmospherically intimate and traditional locations.

Freeman's London was, in his words, 'not a landscape (rooftops, panoramas, etc) but rather a shifting complex of visual experiences', that were kinetic evidence of a mobile population in traffic. Freeman's photographs were published in the year of Colin Buchanan's Government report on towns and motor transport; metropolitan and urban culture seemed to be in passage, moving towards a city experienced as a speedy

Robert Freeman,
Park Lane,
1961

Herbert Spencer,
Minicab in Park Lane,
1961

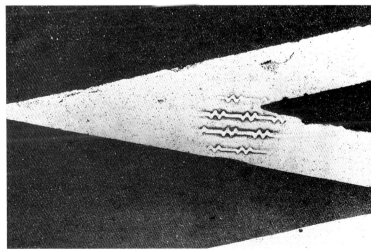

Robert Freeman,
Roadmarking,
1961

Gordon House,
Triple Square, 1961
Enamel on board,
132 x 106 cm
Artist's collection

Opposite:
Archigram,
Living City Survival Kit,
1963

patterning of abrupt signs – Freeman's 'shifting complex'. Freeman had encountered Robert Frank, together with several Beat writers, in New York in 1959, and Frank's oblique, motor-borne, 'unfinished' photographs[9] may lie (as another example of American foundations) below Freeman's figuring of London. This registered the city as a set of traces – of indexical signs – of human passage at speed across a telescoped, telephotoed textured cityscape. Tail-fins of Cadillacs in Eaton Square were set at a tilted angle; graphic close-ups of anamorphic lettering from road markings were over-printed with tyre tracks; a de-focused, blurred silhouette of a man's head stood before a street map; a street 'strong-man' posed, covered in tattoos. These photographs also offered an archaeology of markers of avant-garde London taste – respectively, Independent Group Americanophilia; 'Situation's' elementary sign abstractions; Paris-based *Situationnisme*; and finally the tenacious heritage of Dubuffet.[10]

In the first week in July 1961, Freeman photographed Theo Crosby's International Union of Architects Congress (IUAC) buildings on the South Bank for *Architectural Design* maga-zine,[11] with their externally lettered walls by Edward Wright. These were 'super-graphics' like Denny's *Austin Reed Mural*, with bold, polychrome lettering, and they proclaimed an allu-sive, broken, permutational style that would, amongst other precedents, prefigure the studio set decorations for the ITV programme *Ready Steady Go!*, two years later. For these pho-tographs at the IUAC did more than record the site: the IUAC, with its theme of architecture and technology, became, in Freeman's rendering, a zone of London that had been utterly modernised. The future resembled a space station superim-posed against established London backdrops. Richard Hamilton's *Glorious Techniculture* indicted the new Shell Tower aligned behind it, in an extension of its teetering high-rise iconography, by Freeman. In the western courtyard the spires of the Houses of Parliament peeped over the modernist stock-ade's tautly painted and taped asbestolux decorations by the 'Situation' artists, Bernard Cohen, Peter Stroud and John Plumb. Here, a new London of hard-edged colour signs is jux-taposed with an older one of Victorian neo-Gothic; just that rhetoric of deliberate anachronism that was to feature as a hall-mark of the later, much mythologised 'Swinging London' (as in the cover of *Time*'s 'Swinging' issue where contrast is made between Big Ben, the Palace of Westminster and the poly-chrome geometrical patterned clothing of Londoners in the foreground).

Richard Smith returned to London that summer from New York, after his Harkness Fellowship had come to an end. New York had taken him out of the bohemian 'Notting Hill ambiance',[12] but on his return he moved to the East End, to Bath Street, into a large ex-industrial space. He was probably the first of the London avant-garde to move east into such post-industrial studio spaces, followed by Clive Barker in Bath Street, and Gerald Laing, a year later, colonising ex-rag trade rooms in Fournier Street. Freeman began to make a film about Smith – *Trailer* – which was first shown at the ICA in November 1962. Just as Cézanne had taken his finished canvases out into the country to see if they could maintain themselves in

56

Roger Mayne,
Trafalgar Square, c.1960
Mary Evans Picture Library

The early novels of Colin MacInnes, *Absolute Beginners* (1959) and *City of Spades* (1957), turned their attention to West London, where many of the avant-garde artists and critics lived, the London of Notting Hill and Westbourne Grove. MacInnes represented this part of West London as 'Napoli', set apart as if an 'other', labyrinthine and southern mediterranean place.

Roger Mayne,
Southam Street,
1957
Mary Evans Picture Library

Stephen Willats,
**Homeostat Drawing
no 1**, 1969
Pencil on paper,
56 x 71 cm
Artist's collection

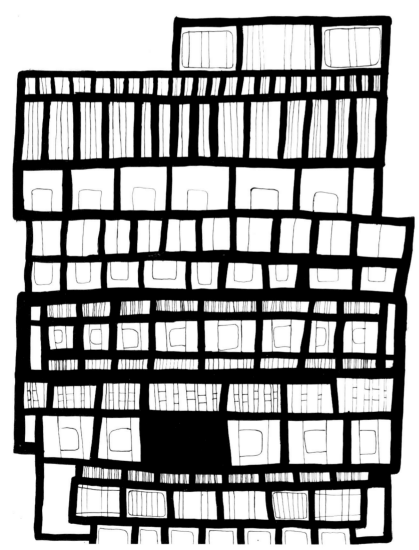

Stephen Willats,
Tower block exercise, 1963
Ink on card, 63 x 50 cm
Artist's collection

nature, so Freeman took Smith's paintings onto EC1 streets, 'separated from the camera by a road, so traffic kept flashing past, too near to be in focus'.[13] Smith, as much as Freeman, had been aware of the new experience of the city and the role that velocity and photography had played in all this. Just before his move to New York, Smith had written a catalogue text for his friend, the painter and graphic artist, Gordon House. In this he vividly described House's perceptions during commuting when 'the landscape has been burnt out by speed'.[14]

A new urbanist myth took possession of the Alloway-ICA circle in the late Fifties and it was present in 'Situation' and in the linked journal, *Gazette*. House likened his hard-edged enamel paintings, which he showed at the second New London Situation exhibition in August and September 1961, to urban signs, 'an indicator ... (seen) *en route* within peripheral vision as an LTE [London Transport Executive] district sign or a triple spaced ad on a hoarding site'.[15] The area of 'information development' was beginning to concern graphic designers – the graphic facilitation of consumer access to instant information based on the findings of perceptual psychology. Smith had written of House's paintings in 1959: 'It is as if they had only a second to register, like signs on the new motorways'.[16] This was a governmental concern, too. In December 1961 the Worboys Committee was established by the Ministry of Transport to devise a new unitary system of traffic signs, recruiting Jock Kinneir and Margaret Calvert to draw them; the uniform system, which was subsequently recommended in the spring of 1963, is still in use today.[17]

Metropolitan experience could be sampled through assemblages of badges, ephemera, small symptomatic objects, that were joined in the (male) collage imagination as a 'kit' – as Archigram pointed out, 'for boys at heart'.[18] For the London avant-garde this was perhaps first seen clearly in Alan Fletcher's 'Letter from America' in *ARK* No. 19, in 1957.[19] Subverting the sententiousness of Alistair Cooke's BBC Radio reports, Fletcher rifled through the textures and ephemera of New York, paralleling *Hommage à Chrysler Corp*, predictive of Hamilton's 'Urbane Image' text of 1963. Fletcher's trophies constituted the small change of vernacular design culture and in 1963 the Archigram team of experimental architects drew up a similar sample for material life in London. They put together emblematic commodities, consumer items with a potentially wider gender spectrum – a 'Living City Survival Kit' on the occasion of their 'Living City' exhibition at the ICA in June and July.[20] Resolutely banal items of metropolitan existence such as Daz and Wonderloaf were spread out next to arcane objects such as Ornette Coleman and John Coltrane jazz LPs. This spread of products followed the generic women's magazine special features on gifts – such as 'Hockney's Christmas Presents', a similar assemblage with captions louchely letrasetted (as Archigram would do) by Hockney for *Harpers Bazaar*, in its December 1962 issue. The city and the culture were defined by their special commodities, but for Archigram the trivia constituting the metropolis was accorded a new weight. 'In the Living City all are important: the triviality of lighting a cigarette, or the hard fact of moving 2 million commuters a day. In fact they are equal – as facts of the shared experience of the city'.[21]

As well as inclusive democratic gestures, Archigram's 'Living City' addressed the future through photomontage of models of a de-materialised architecture drawn from science fiction and the molecular structure of the polio virus, which they dubbed 'The Thing'. Superimposing a model metal net,[22] (decked out with transistors) upon derelict industrial space, their utopian technology was made to share strange company, juxtaposed with the depths of a nuclear explosion. But this lapse into catastrophism apart, Archigram essentially imagined an urban space of drifting pockets of subjectivity. Freeman's photograph of a blurred man's head in front of a defocussed street map was visible on the Archigram pin-board, selected as a cult image.[23] Freeman's 'shifting complex', his passage of cars and human traces, has its analogue in Archigram's 'Situation Change': 'the fluctuating come and go of people and things over a time scale ... the happenings within spaces in cities, the transient throw-away objects, the passing presence of cars and people are as important, possibly more important than the built demarcation of space'. [24]

London was imagined in change – as a flux of human patterning of situations and as a transformed built space. The early novels of Colin MacInnes, *Absolute Beginners* (1959) and *City of Spades* (1957), turned their attention to West London, where many of the avant-garde artists and critics also lived, the London of Notting Hill and Westbourne Grove. Afro-Caribbean culture was an 'other' space, making this area a marginal 'liminal zone', a space for a 'social anti-structure'[25], where 'new combinations of cultural givens could be playfully tested ... a space for utopian ... transformations'.[26] MacInnes represented this part of West London as 'Napoli', set apart as if an other, labyrinthine and southern Mediterranean place. When Ralph Rumney, the painter and (briefly) the only English member of the *Situationniste International*, constructed an elaborate urban game for *ARK* No. 24, in 1958, it was set in Venice. Rumney's 'Psychogeography of Venice', published as 'The Leaning Tower of Venice' in *ARK*,[27] followed an American Beat author, Alan Ansen – alias 'A' – through the medieval street plan. The narrative turned into a kind of *Goon Show* version of a holiday snap-shot album, until hero 'A' disappeared, just before he encountered Alloway on the Rialto bridge. Seeking to detect how playful dimensions could be found in the urban scene, Rumney wondered: 'It is our thesis that cities should embody a built-in play factor. We are studying here a play environment relationship ... But how would 'A' play in London?'[28] Situationist concepts of the contingencies of the city, and the paramount freedom of the individual to move and play at will, became crucial. In the Brutalist interests of the Smithsons and the related pictures of children playing in Bethnal Green by Nigel Henderson, the iconography of the street as structured by play was a cardinal factor. In Roger Mayne's Notting Hill photographs of the late Fifties a similar focus on games in the urban environment also emerged in the context of a perceived freeing of social relations in the district. To his own question, 'But how would 'A' play in London ?', Rumney was to propose an extraordinary answer with his work on and around the ICA's 'Place' exhibition in September 1959.

Ralph Rumney,
The Leaning Tower of Venice,
ARK No.24, 1958

Gordon House
Richard Smith, text for Gordon House exhibition of paintings, New Vision Centre Gallery, Summer 1959

Gordon House works in graphics for a company in Welwyn Garden City – he commutes from London daily.

His paintings are like the momentarily in-focus forms of the daily recurring landmarks of the Kings Cross–Welwyn Garden City route. The bright white space in which they exist is a non-atmospheric dazzle: the landscape has been burnt out by speed. The images are not loaded with associations but are a painter's painted shape; the landmarks' significance to the commuter is: '20 minutes to Welwyn Garden City' or '10 minutes to Finsbury Park' or 'time for another beer'. Questions 'Why are they there?', ' What do they mean?' never arise. The multiple times they are seen do not add depth to the view.

The image in House's painting is big within the canvas area, over-exposed, making it loom toward one, close as a tunnel wall. It is as if they had only a second to register, like signs on the new motorways.

The period was already framed by the TV screen and, to a lesser extent, the cinema screen. Whether it was possible to gain access to an actual world beyond this media 'spectacle', an access to the life-world and the ground of existence, concerned several artists. At times the metaphoric media frame became a literal one. On a bombsite to the west of Notting Hill, early in 1964, Mark Boyle and Joan Hills found a way of organising their 'Junk' epiphanies

Mark Boyle and Joan Hills,
Noland Road Study (detail), 1964
Mixed media, 81 x 59 x 15 cm
Artists' collection

62

'Place' Exhibition, ICA, 1959

Robyn Denny,
Place Painting, 1959
Oil on canvas, 213 x 183 cm
Artist's collection

'They hang the pictures on the floor'

Phillip King,
Window piece, 1960–61
Plaster, 152 x 122 x 38 cm
Artist's collection

reminiscent of Daniel Spoerri's contemporary 'Snares' – from found debris. They used the framing edge of a rectangular plastic fillet – 'used to hold the screen of a TV in place'[1] – thrown randomly across the derelict cityscape; where it fell and what it framed became the site of their art work, as in *Norland Road Study* (1964). For his Indica Gallery exhibition in July 1966, Boyle distributed white card frames for spectators to hold against the London view. Just as the Surrealists had regarded Paris as a cryptogram to be deciphered, so artists like the Boyles and Ralph Rumney, members of the London 'Underground' (before and after it was named as such), envisioned a London revealed by chance, games and revels. From 1957 Rumney had begun a series of conversations with Alloway discussing an exhibition project for the ICA that would examine choice, feedback and the environment of a circumscribed urban place, which terminated in 'Place' in September 1959, when Rumney showed with Denny and Smith.

Rumney had been fascinated by the form of the bow-edged, rectangular-shaped screen since the early Fifties, and the collage heads of Enrico Baj, of Dubuffet and Cycladic figurines further provoked this interest for him.[2] The screen motif structured the paintings that he contributed to 'Place' and 'Situation', in 1960, turning them into ambiguous forms with bi-polar colour, images which thematised looking and viewing. They incorporated an internal framing edge which ambivalently divided and at the same time condensed the world. The 'screen' also seemed to denote a silhouetted, stylised spectator's head, placed in the same giant field, a place where figure and ground played and switched over: 'I was obsessed with environments and the way pictures functioned as environments'.[3] The space this image generated was itself ambiguous; like Pollock's paintings, while it was displayed vertically, at right angles to the floor, it still owed its being to the flat ground. Rumney's 'Heads' culminated, after these London shows, with the golden, magisterial *Head on Floor*, replete with references to tiled hallways where a sliding silhouette head comes to rest on the floor. But what was significant was the revolving of spatial orientation down, towards the ground and a sample of private or civic environment framed for viewing: that realm of Boyle's discarded floorings and debris or else Don McCullin's stones and splinters of urban combat at home or abroad. 'They hang the pictures on the floor',[4] ran a popular press representation of the ICA 'Place' assembly of clustered paintings in maze formation which were laid directly onto the ground in 1959. Yet as Robert Koudielka pointed out later, 'Place' anticipated Caro and St. Martin's dethronement of sculpture from its plinth, prophesying the art object's irreducible grounding in the world.[5]

For Alloway and for Roger Coleman the referent was the cinema, specifically the spacious magnificence of the recent Cinemascope format which, with other wide-screen forms, became in Richard Hamilton's words, a 'physical, almost visceral involvement'.[6] For three years Coleman and Alloway had pursued the analogies between Cinemascope and the large picture sizes of Action painting. Smith's canvases, Coleman had written in 1957, could be understood as a 'conquest of space' (an allusion to the stratospheric explorations of Col.

Peter Everest): 'the real key is the Cinemascope screen where one's experience of space is more expansive than on smaller screens'.[7] William Green always sat on the first row at Cinemascope performances, awestruck by the disintegration of forms.[8] Alloway had seen in the Cinemascope frame a 'breakdown of the conventional limits between the symbol and the consumer',[9] and therefore a binding together, as in Rumney's seven feet high canvases, of subject (the delegated spectatorial head) and object. This dream of recovered unity and oneness, an end to distance, access to and rapturous reconciliation of body and space would become the prospectus underpinning much sculpture, painting and environment-based art through the Sixties.

It was the mental and physical environments of the mass media that Coleman found prompting Rumney, Smith and Denny in their 'Place' work. These influences centred on the linking, the spatial suturing, of consumer to the object or commodity. 'Place' was 'a direct offshoot of 'an Exhibit' '[10] an environmental constructivist show dividing space by coloured perspex panels – a forerunner of Agis and Jones' 'Space' of 1964–65 – which had been staged by Richard Hamilton and Victor Pasmore at the ICA in August 1957. 'Are you maze-smart?' asked 'an Exhibit's' catalogue, utilising the language of ITV's new quiz programmes as a tactic to 'dramatically involve the visitor'.[11] The figure of audience participation in the teasing maze of paintings that were laid out in 'Place' and the game-show analogies were uppermost in Rumney and Alloway's minds. Besides his Situationism, Rumney had an almost Duchamp-esque interest in the applicability of games, and he proposed to 'divide the floor into squares of a convenient size for one person to stand in. Some of these squares should be blocked by pictures or written information or obstacles. The player would be required to find a route through this maze'.[12] He proposed deploying the new devices of consumer management: a spectator questionnaire, the use of subliminal cues, as well as 'Talking-jag' discussion groups that would enable the methodologies of US Motivation Research to be applied to visitors.[13] Alloway tried to disentangle Rumney's Situationist claims for the exhibition as a 'constructed situation', one that would auto-destruct the techniques of the consumer spectacle, from other – primarily pictorial – origins of 'Place'. These he reckoned in terms of 'the pleasures and traps of the spectator syndrome at present so characteristic of British aesthetics ...'[14] This identification of playful avant-garde aims by Alloway again marks a fundamental shift in the culture of the period; again it supplements and sets the agenda for the Sixties.

As the new decade began Phillip King completed a sculpture which brought together the captivating imagery of viewing through a looking device with an emphasis on a renewed belief in the absolute authenticity of certain objects and their existence in the world. *Window piece* (1960–1), with its rectangular aperture and chamfered plaster sides, frames the world and bids spectators to gaze through it, but it stands as a real 'thing', sitting on the ground – not set apart by a plinth – comforting the homeless imagination in the middle of the contemporary spectacle: it suggested to King 'a hearth',[15] a home of the most

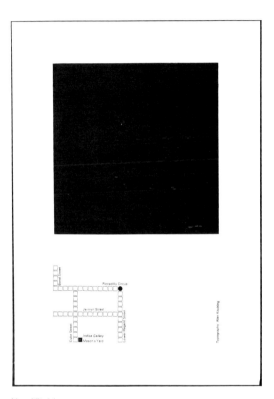

Alan Kitching,
Mark Boyle exhibition,
invitation card design for Indica Gallery, 1966

Peter Blake,
Gold Leaf Painting, 1960
Gold leaf on canvas, 79 x 59 cm
Private collection

Ralph Rumney,
Head on Floor, 1963
Oil on canvas, 190 x 160 cm
Jane England Gallery

William Turnbull,
Aphrodite, 1958
Bronze, 190 x 50 x 74 cm
Artist's collection

elementary kind. King announces the quiet irruption of a certain strand of French philosophical thinking into the making of art in London in the Sixties, particularly the existential and phenomenological strands of Heidegger and Husserl. (This would be felt, as well, in the sculpture and theories of William Tucker and Tim Scott.) In the autumn of 1960, King had returned from Greece with an almost Nietzschean view of Greek art and culture; the possibility of sublime, affirmative artefacts that arose spontaneously, 'so naturally out of the environment'.[16] (Allen Jones is another contemporary 'yea-sayer' who looked to Nietzsche's Zarathustra for sublimity and the annihilation of custom and difference). Across a wall of his home in Hampstead he squared up a late Matisse cut-out of a great tree from *Verve* magazine, painting it quickly. In his attic studio, cleansed with white paint on his return from Greece, he made *Window piece*; his domestic environment of interior walls and studio space seemed to signify a coming together of elements from a Heideggerian sense of 'dwelling' or else from the topos of the room, in Gaston Bachelard's recently published and influential *La Poétique de l'Espace* (1958). Here was another 'place', no longer alienated or distant. Exactly contemporary with this moment for King, Bernard Cohen began painting assured lintel, doorway and fireplace images, filled with the 'excitement of the domestic' on an heroic easel painting scale,[17] one that would stamp an identity on 'Situation' of another kind of 'place'.

'New painting is nomadic', claimed Peter Hobbs at the outset of his contribution to the debate on art and site. His article 'Image and Environment' in 1959[18] presented painting at a utopian point, at the end of millennia during which man had been 'confined to the surface of the planet'.[19] In a prefiguration of the schemes of the Archigram architects, and the Event-Structure Research Group of the late Sixties, Hobbs imagined a civic future inside flexible, organic structures, complete with weather-control. Yet painting was currently unwanted; it was, in his view, on a limbo edge of history, nomadic. It was to make a film dramatising this tragic spirit of pictorial liminality and homelessness that the photographer Don McCullin first contacted Hobbs in 1959. The stills he made, for rostrum camera work, were taken over a fortnight, and are remarkable in their mobilising of images of pathos. Hobbs' pictures had become free-standing, often double-sided, and were emancipated from the wall – McCullin took them out onto bombsites, arranging them on matching sight-lines with ruined industrial buildings and in front of blackened East End terraces and in grimy backyards. He placed them in a disconsolate inner-city zone, in what would become the familiar terrain of the Boyles. McCullin had recently come to fame in *The Observer* through his photographs of a Teddy Boy gang scowling in a derelict house; it was in this mode that he photographed Hobbs in a schoolyard, making gigantic chalk graffiti, 'environmental drawings', or discussing one of his small pictograph canvases with a navvy; his romanticism of urban displacement was powerful.

Hobbs wished to return painting to a form of expressionist metaphysics. He found in the new regime at the Royal Court Theatre and its productions of Ibsen a model of expressionist poetic content which was wholly at odds with the drift of current critical thinking. In *North of Brand* (1960) – the title

Peter Hobbs,
**North of
Metaphysics,**
1960
Oil on canvas,
183 x 152 cm
Private collection

Don McCullin,
Photograph of Peter Hobbs
with a Workman, 1959

Don McCullin,
Photograph of a Peter Hobbs
painting in a bombsite, 1959

refers to Ibsen's play of the same name – and *North of
Metaphysics* (1960) varieties of metaphysical vistas arise as
they do in Rothko's paintings of the mid-1940s, as surrogate
bleak landscapes. Although he had pioneered, with his free-
standing pictures, an important initiative in what was to
become a central issue of Sixties art – the interface between
sculpture and painting – Hobbs felt no small contempt for for-
malist versions of contemporary art, preferring what Anton
Ehrenzweig, his mentor and champion, called 'poemagogic
art'.[20] Ehrenzweig made a case for Hobbs' art as dissenting
from the emerging dominance of that 'enveloping US (pictorial)
space'[21] which Coleman and Alloway had theorised. Citing the
psychoanalytical theory of Kleinian 'object relations',
Ehrenzweig saw him as treading 'dangerous ground'[22] by
dealing with unconscious fantasies of internal (and maternal)
spaces. This poetic and psychoanalytic outlook made him sus-
picious of the 'Situation' painters: Hobbs was promised a
simultaneous exhibition of his sculpture at the ICA by Alloway,
but he pulled out of the first 'Situation' show at the RBA
Galleries at the last minute, and ejected into a nomadic career.

Text for PLACE
Roger Coleman, ICA, 1959

PLACE is not an exhibition of the work of three painters in the accepted sense, neither is it an experiment in arranging paintings nor an exercise in exhibition design.

PLACE is a collaborative expression of certain ideas common to the three painters on the relationship between painting and the spectator.

PLACE is an environment.

Background 1
The Mass Media.

A significant development in post war art in this country (it appears to be exclusively English) is the acceptance on the part of some of the younger artists of the mass media as a legitimate body of reference. This can be seen, for instance, in the allusions to Science Fiction and monster lore in the sculpture of Paolozzi, in McHale's ikons on consumption and in Blake's collages of pop heroes.

In the work of the three painters of PLACE, the influence of the mass media is present but not generally detectable without the aid of outside cues (sometimes the titles of the paintings are sufficient). The mass media for Denny, Rumney and Smith is not a source of imagery, as it is for Blake, but a source of ideas that act as stimuli and as orientation in a cultural continuum. They are concerned with the environment – mental and physical – that the mass media makes up and this sense of environment affects their outlook and activity as painters. Important is the idea of participation in this environment, for example, the movies – *Cinemascope*, Cinerama (note Rumney's *Cinemascope* heads).

The identification with the environment of the mass media is a significant aesthetic decision for these painters.

Background 2
American Painting and Space.

One example, among others, American painting has had for the painters of PLACE is in the use of the big canvas. In the work of Pollock, Rothko, Newman, Still, space tends to be a direct function of the size of the painting surface and it has been called environmental. The surface is preserved as a surface and activity occurs over it vertically and horizontally expanding outwards to the four edges rather than from the edges to the centre. Thus the spectator, when he views the painting looks over it rather than at it; the painting expands into his space so that it becomes for the duration of looking his environment (majestically demonstrated for example in Pollock's *Blue Poles*).

The aspirations of the painters of PLACE are towards a space of this kind. For them it demands the participation of the spectator, and the concept of participation figures largely in their working programme. (It should be pointed out however, that this is a flexible concept and the individual attitudes of the three towards it are not the same either in kind or degree). Further they make a connection between this level of participation and the participation demanded by the environment of the mass media (again this appears to be an exclusively English development).

Background 3
The Game Environment

The idea of spectator participation stemming from the mass media on the one hand, and fine art sources, like American painting, on the other, has lead the painters of PLACE to an interest in ludic or game participation. (This applies more to Denny and Rumney than to Smith). Game participation exists on two levels, 1, the interpretation of the painting/spectator relationship as a game situation in which the painter's features, marks, etc., are moves within a strategy which in turn elicits a 'strategy' from the spectator, and 2, on a more literal level where the spectator is invited to manipulate the work (example, Denny's experiments with paintings with moveable parts like a Chinese puzzle) or an environment constructed as a maze in which the spectator in finding his way through the maze is 'playing' against the artist (example, Rumney's experiments with maze environments).

PLACE, then, represents interests in A, environment in a general sense, B, the environment of the mass media, C, an environmental space in painting, and D, the concept of participation explicit in A and B and implicit in C.

Rules of PLACE

PLACE is an environment made from the paintings of three artists and organised by certain rules decided upon by the painters before the painting began. The rules, chosen for the sake of unity, as cues for the spectator or participant, and for organizational simplicity, are as follows:

SIZE
7ft x 6ft and 7ft x 4ft
7ft x 6ft was chosen as the standard size as it is just larger than man-size at full stretch and therefore large enough for handling in mounting and dismounting the exhibition. The smaller size was chosen later to give a greater overall diversity.

COLOUR
Red, Green, Black, White (used singly or in any permutation).
The colours were chosen more or less arbitrarily by the painters but complementaries were thought to be most useful in the context. A colour control was accepted to provide a thread the spectator can follow through the exhibition and to allow each painter's approach to a similar problem to register clearly.

ORGANIZATION
The paintings are arranged diagonally across the gallery to give four main vistas – one for each painter and one common with black and white paintings (see plan).
The painters agreed to paint as near to their normal work as possible and to make no radical departures from their usual procedure, but because the works were done in series and with certain controls, new developments appeared.

People and PLACE

The spectator is invited to participate in PLACE as an environment while recognizing that the objects that comprise it are paintings in their own right and no different from paintings arranged in a conventional way. Participation is capable on different levels, A, the individual painting, B, the work of one of the artists, C, the work of all three artists together (black and white view) and D, random samplings from the exhibition as a whole. PLACE can be looked at, through, over, between, in or out.

West London in the Early 60s
Mark Boyle from *Boyle Family in New Zealand* 1990

(...). It's anguish for any body who gets kicked out of their house, and with their memories and associations it's also anguish for artists. But we didn't just get kicked out of houses, we were thrown off the demolition sites and bomb sites and junk heaps that we used as studios. We were desperately poor at that time, Joan making £3 a week plus tips as a chef. I was making £1 a week plus tips as a head waiter. Of course £1 bought more in those days, but not that much more. By the standards of the time we were very poor and apart from the clothes we wore to work we just had rags.

We worked on these old bomb sites where houses had been blasted away during the war. The surface of London was pockmarked with such sites and in the early sixties, when they started to rebuild, the first move was usually to knock down everything that still stood around them. To us it seemed like a kind of alternative London where people could be free; and in these places, in our rags and with no place else to work, like refugees we picked through the rubbish and made pictures and sculptures. Sometimes the police came. Once they accused us of stealing the tiny fragments of rusty metal and glass we had incorporated in a picture. I pointed out that they were to put down the value of the 'stolen property' on the charge sheet and that no magistrate would look kindly on someone being charged with stealing something of no value from an unknown person whose house had been blown away twenty years before.

(...)

More and more during the months that followed our beautiful parks/demolition sites were fenced off and we were driven away with nothing to mark our family's passing except an occasional mist of tears and a few pictures and sculptures that we get a chance to see from time to time, rusting away beautifully in their museum. But right then, just as that golden era was coming to an end and they were closing down, or even worse, rebuilding, the last sites in our area, there was one final magic moment. It was a sweet grey day with a hint of rain in the air and Joan and I were staring at a frame lying on all this junk at a bombsite, one of those rectangular grey plastic fillets that used to hold the screen of a TV in place. It seemed to us that the arrangement of earth now inside the frame was absolutely perfect. We thought it was maybe the fact of framing that made it seem so right, so we tried moving the frame to see if it worked elsewhere. No matter where we placed it, it looked wrong, precious or contrived. Eventually it occurred to us that the reason the original site seemed perfect could be that it was natural, because it had just happened like that. So we threw the frame away across the site and wandered over curiously to see what we would find. Again, it was perfect. We spent the rest of that day taking turns and alternately placing the frame deliberately and throwing it away; and every time we placed it, it looked wrong and every time we threw it, it looked just right. I still cannot really say why that should have been so, but over the next few weeks and months and years we tried many different kinds of frames, different shapes, different sizes, and the random principle always worked. Eventually we found a way of fixing the images we found inside. Then we invented a series of techniques that should enable us to make a 'picture' of what we found inside the frame, not just on the junk site but in theory anywhere.

After some stumbling beginnings in the Shepherd's Bush area, we drew a plot a mile square on the map of London with our flat as the centre. We then threw 100 darts into this area on the map and began a project to make a 'picture' on each of these 100 sites. We were working on this project when we got thrown out of our flat. Usually we were chucked out because the owner or the agents thought we were turning their property into a junkyard or feared the walls wouldn't support the weight of the works or something. This time they were pulling the house down to make a roundabout. You can still see the place (...)

Though poorly attended, 'Situation' was one of only a handful of exhibitions of contemporary British painting in the twentieth century to have profoundly re-shaped the direction and expectations of art in Britain. The name was an abbreviation of the phrase 'the situation in London now',[1] and it declared an open stance: the show was to encompass a plurality of artists and styles around the essential criteria of abstract paintings no smaller than

William Turnbull,
25/1959, 1959
Oil on canvas, 254 x 190 cm
Artist's collection

76

Robert Freeman,
Photograph of Lawrence Alloway with
Sylvia Sleigh's portrait of the Situation Group,
1961

thirty square feet in size. It represented a challenge to existing systems of showing contemporary art because its organisation stood outside established institutions. From Alloway's intuition – 'I'm sure there are people out there painting large abstract paintings outside the *status quo*'[2] – came the decision, in William Turnbull's words, 'for artists to take their destiny into their own hands ...'[3] 'It was an attempt that succeeded for a time in showing that critics and dealers and museum directors are not the only people who create values in art'.[4] Attacked as ' "Alloway's team" – being without the favour of the good graces of the Establishment ...',[5] the exhibitors refused to accept any group identity foisted upon them and some felt uneasy about the portrait of the exhibitors which Sylvia Sleigh painted in July 1961 (for the 'New London Situation' exhibition) which might have implied a shared group status. Their refusal to accept a unitary identity for promotional purposes in 1960–1 contrasts with the promotion surrounding Bryan Robertson's later 'New Generation' exhibition in May 1964.[6] At the opening of 'New Generation' – which was televised live – the 'Situation' artists present were allegedly asked to leave at the moment BBC-TV began coverage of the event.

One aspect of their drive for self-management took the form of a determination to consolidate their attitude of anti-amateurism and anti-parochialism, they would take the role of art-professionals: 'a reliable criteria of professionalism is something that occurred long since in Paris and in the 1940s in New York. In London it has been lacking ...', Alloway pointed out.[7] The enemies were still 'the pastoral, bohemian and establishment patterns',[8] the residual culture of amateurism, that was lambasted by the Cohen brothers, Denny, Kitaj, Roy Ascott and William Turnbull in their celebrated letter to the *Sunday Times* in June 1963.[9] The idea of the necessarily 'tough-minded'[10] peer group of artist professionals was uppermost in Turnbull's mind after encountering it in New York during his visit there in the spring of 1957. The ICA provided, under Alloway and Coleman, a certain forum for artists, particularly the 'Talk' sessions, fabled for the abrasiveness of their discussions in the early Sixties: 'A certain amount of hostility (on the part of the artists) was necessary'.[11] The 'Situation' assault on amateurism and bohemianism extended also to dress codes: the smartly besuited American Abstract Expressionist such as Gottlieb – 'looking like a business-man from the rag trade'[12] – or Guston or Motherwell was an impressive sight to a London avant-garde already keen to emulate the Ivy League style (as in Howard Hodgkin's painting *Mr and Mrs Robyn Denny*, 1960) or the Cecil Gee 'Madison Avenue' look of tough, slick executives, which Gordon House 'modelled'. This form of resolute self-fashioning was exemplified by Alloway and Coleman. They bought their clothes at Austins, near the Lyric Theatre on Shaftesbury Avenue, a menswear shop that imported snappy grey Dacron suits from the US, although Turnbull had returned with an electric blue gangster suit from New York itself.

From 1957 and into 1958, Turnbull had combined his experiences of New York painting with Mathieu and an equal respect for Japanese panel paintings. Works such as *Black Painting* (1957), *11/58* and *29/58* (both of 1958) have a big-

Sylvia Sleigh,
Portrait of the Situation Group, 1961
Oil on linen, 122 x 183 cm
Artist's collection
Left to right (back row):
Henry Mundy,
Gwyther Irwin,
William Turnbull,
Peter Coviello;
(centre row)
Gillian Ayres,
John Plumb,
Peter Stroud,
Robyn Denny,
Roger Coleman,
Bernard Cohen;
(front row)
Gordon House,
Lawrence Alloway.

SITUATION
AN EXHIBITION OF BRITISH ART

Gordon House,
Logo and Letterhead for **Situation**,
1960

Anon., Photgraph of Gordon House in a Cecil Gee suit,
1957

Opposite: Gordon House, catalogue cover design for **Situation**, 1962

scale monochrome presence, painted with palette knife accents across large black and white areas. The culture of Action painting and its Eastern antecedents was strong and Turnbull felt that his paintings owed much 'to Japanese techniques of long meditation on painting before the act – then painted very quickly'.[13] At the Central School where he taught, Turnbull was revered as an 'active teacher'[14] by students and colleagues who then were drawn into the 'Situation' exhibition – Brian Young, John Epstein, Peter Hobbs (abortively) and Peter Coviello. 'Situation' was open to the Action painting of William Green and Gillian Ayres, but by 1959 Turnbull had shifted to a more diluted, less thickly painted surface that had repeated coverings to produce a flat, saturated field of colour, in Alloway's words 'flat and bodiless as a dye so that the tangibility of the cloth is perceived'.[15]

Ahead of Caro's discovery of Noland's stained canvases, Turnbull had hit upon the bodiless, miraculous field of colour that stood as a pure object. That year he painted the great orange and red diagonal field painting *25/59* that towered up over eight feet in 'Situation'. Such flat colour-field works unnerved humanist critics such as Stephen Spender, who detected 'stasis'[16] when he recalled the supposed dynamism of pre-war abstraction. But Turnbull, after his tachist monochromes of 1957–8, was seeking simple zones of colour, like Rumney in his bi-polar paintings. As he had written in 1959, 'I'd like to make one saturated field of colour, so that you wouldn't feel that you were short of all the others'.[17] In an article by the US inventor, Edwin Land, in *Astounding Science Fiction* in May 1959, which was much discussed in the Alloway circle,[18] the necessity for three complementary colours was queried and in this way Turnbull found a possible rationale for avoiding their use in his monochromes. The 'stasis' complaint, the *horror vacui* that overcame Spender in front of these radically simplified pictures was a reaction that puzzled Turnbull, a reaction which he subsequently traced to a Western cultural prejudice against absence. It was, he reckoned, 'the English lack of ability to isolate an object, their horror at having to face the thing ... they lack a sense of 'thing-ness' '.[19] That the newly defined, mono or bi-coloured, phenomenal 'thing', which ambiguously asserted itself as art object, had an actively subversive agency was a point on which 'Situation' painters such as Turnbull shared a position with St. Martin's sculptors like King, who wanted a spectator of his work to 'stand aghast' before the unclassifiable object.[20] In the early summer of 1961 it was Turnbull who insisted that Caro's 'unreadable' but epochal move into coloured metal sculpture be represented in the 'New London Situation' exhibition with *Sculpture 1* (1961). The recognition of a completely different range of experiences for the beholder in the changed environmental space that constituted the frame of the new art had been presaged by the concerns of 'Place'. Michael Chalk, writing six months before 'Situation' about Brian Young's paintings, judged them 'spectator-conscious'.[20] As early as 1956 he had been primed to the changed relationship of painter and spectator to large abstract paintings by Smith. At the RCA Smith had recommended to him a statement by Rothko: 'The reason I paint them (large pictures)... is precisely because I want to be very intimate and

Situation

Arts Council 1962-63

An exhibition of recent British abstract art

Gillian Ayres
Bernard Cohen
Harold Cohen
Peter Coviello
Robyn Denny
John Epstein
Peter Hobbs
Gordon House
John Hoyland
Gwyther Irwin
Robert Law
Henry Mundy
John Plumb
Richard Smith
Peter Stroud
William Turnbull
Marc Vaux
Brian Young

Richard Smith,
WADO, 1961
Oil on canvas, 198 x 183 cm
Artist's collection

Peter Coviello,
Installation photograph of **Situation**,
1960, showing paintings by Harold
Cohen, John Epstein and Gillian Ayres

human. To paint a small picture is to place yourself outside your experience ... However you paint the larger picture you are in it, it isn't something you command'.[22] This was a basic given of Caro's new working procedures in making his large steel sculpture from 1960 – being up close, in a relatively small space – inside the existential space of fabrication rather than outside it. Optical proximity to the paintings in 'Situation' was a key issue for the painters and their accompanying critics, Coleman and Alloway. The paintings, observed closely, were to be scanned physically, with neck motor action rather than with eye movements. The body of the spectator was wholly incorporated because – as with the Monets at the Tate retrospective in 1957 – 'the paintings encircle you'.[23] Instead of fixed, distant views, the spectator took the free-floating consumer's mobility – what Alloway called a 'permissiveness of viewing distances'[24] – and looked in 'close-up and from various oblique angles'.[25] One of the exhibitors, Peter Coviello, took a series of 35mm colour installation shots of the show which did exactly this in the form of a wandering walk – (like the *Situationniste dérive*) – around half-seen and partly framed paintings in the RBA space.

Perambulating through this environment of radiant colour spaces entailed a search for analogies by Alloway; Smith's *WADO* in 'New London Situation' in 1961, was 'marquee scale'[27] and Plumb's PVA tape paintings were compared to medieval banners. In this kind of account the 'Situation' space was, by association, a festive one, filled with single, beautiful emblems. A dialogue came out of this sensual situational gathering of subject and object, a reciprocity of perception and play (which Rumney had desired). As Alloway said, 'An awareness of the world as something that contains both the work of art and the spectator (rather than the romantic notion of the work of art itself as a world) is at the core of the recent developments in London'.[28] In Robyn Denny's paintings, such as *7/1960*, this was metaphorised by the appearance of inset panels and doorways, allusive – though utterly flat – to points of passage, thresholds: 'a dramatisation of the X where spectator and artwork meet'.[29] Such thresholds, like Alice's mirror, led to a non-Euclidian space and Denny had recourse to the science-fiction novels of Alfred Bester, Theodore Sturgeon and Philip K. Dick for images of other mental spaces, as in *Track Four* (1961), where an 'Einsteinian' space of paradoxical dimensions is revealed, facing the quotidiant space of the nimble-witted, game-playing, ideal viewer.

The portal and lintel iconography of Bernard Cohen, like that of King's *Window piece*, Rumney's 'Cinemascope' heads, or Denny's SF panelled doorways to infinity, belonged to a self-reflexive imagery of inquiry into perceptions of space – and perhaps more importantly, of existential place – during this crucial moment of 1960–1. One regular and attentive visitor to Bernard Cohen's shared country house in Hertfordshire at this time was Anthony Caro: his *24 Hours* (1960) is exactly contemporary with Bernard Cohen's *Painting 96*. Both are concerned with framing discs and both rise from the ground to a frontal confrontation with the spectator, 'building without foreground, mid-distance and background, therefore losing all sense of recessional space'.[30] Michael Fried, extending a line of

Robyn Denny,
7/1960, 1960
Oil on canvas,
229 x 137 cm
Artist's collection

argument from Greenberg, would later cite a phenomenological sense of 'presentness' in Caro's work in 1963. Cohen had already arrived at a complex understanding of the European strands of existentialism and phenomenology: what he had admired in Dostoevsky's fiction was the gesture of 'standing in front of the phenomenon'.[31] King's 'aghast' viewer was at one with Cohen's wish to feel 'the shock of confrontation'[32] which, he argued against David Sylvester, figuration could no longer deliver. For Cohen, painting meant acting against the void with an absolute commitment – an existential commitment[33] – that was the requisite of any and all artistic invention. (This would be keenly seen in his spray paintings from 1962.) With *Painting 96* both the painter's and the viewer's bodies stand over against an inviting but daunting site, where a monumental goal for the eyes is established, a double vision of two white targets. But the spectator falls under the guardian vision of these two disc 'eyes'. The Alloway-esque 'pleasures and traps' for the spectator, in this specific case, were found in the equivocal discovery that in the act of looking and attempting to master this vast blue painting, one also confronted an implacable gaze emanating from the picture itself. 'Situation' aesthetics hinged on the reciprocal meeting of the intimate look of the spectator (and his or her body) with paintings that carried with them a kind of self-declaring gaze advertising the 'visibility of the visible'[34] in a banner-like, spectacular display of the imagery of prosceniums, frames and circular eye-forms.[35]

The potential for disquiet apart, Cohen had also established with these pictures of 1960–1 some forceful images of hearth and home through memory traces of youthfully familiar places – of entertainment, cinema façades and seaside architecture that compounded a sense of bliss. A morphology of ordinary-yet-special domestic spaces which Bachelard might have recognised – their symmetries, fittings and fireplaces – arguably pervades Cohen's paintings in the later half of 1960 and into 1961. It is impossible to over-estimate the consequences for the London avant-garde of their use of familiar, domestic-scale space in which to paint at this time. Working space was co-terminus with living space in the period immediately before the annexing of larger post-industrial spaces for separate studio use. The intimate 'Situation' spectator was based upon the intimate maker, who, like Cohen, made ten by twelve foot paintings squashed in ex-bedsit rooms of virtually the same dimensions. (Later in 1961, Cohen, together with Turnbull, Peter Stroud, Mark Vaux and Tess Jaray moved into the Victorian houses of Camden Square in north London through the property development skills of the solicitor Tony Fawkes: the area then becoming known as 'Situation Square').

'Situation' also signified another kind of urban modernity, related to the transformation that the post-war industrial impact of design, and the effect that the expansion of the electronics, plastics and pharmaceutical sectors, had on everyday life. Amongst the 'Situation' painters John Plumb and Gordon House represented this constituency. The bright self-adhesive PVA tapes that Plumb used for his compositions were scavenged from the electronics industry, having being used for 'identifying codes in tangles of wires and cables'.[36] Different bands were quickly applied and then torn off again on Plumb's

Peter Coviello,
Installation photograph of Bernard Cohen's **Painting 96**, 1960,
at the **Situation** exhibition, RBA Galleries

John Plumb,
Ivanhoe, 1962
Oil on canvas, 122 x 122 cm
Tadema Gallery

Roger Coleman,
Photograph of Howard Hodgkin,
1960

They bought their clothes at Austins, near the Lyric Theatre on Shaftesbury Avenue, a menswear shop that imported snappy grey Dacron suits from the US, although Turnbull had returned with an electric blue gangster suit from New York itself.

Howard Hodgkin,
Mr and Mrs Robyn Denny, 1960
Oil on canvas, 91 x 127 cm
Saatchi collection, London

Anon,
Photograph of Roger Coleman,
1959

canvases – Alloway stressed the manner in which Plumb had retained his Action techniques of improvisation and gesture, even without paint. This lineage of Action descending into 'Situation', was obvious, too, in Harold Cohen's canvas collages which were sent from New York where, like Richard Smith, he was on a painting scholarship in 1960. Cohen had cut away different layers of canvas to reveal strata of unpainted horizontal zones. In contrast to these, Plumb's tapes operated as alien agents in amongst traditional art materials. Still, in all their sharp, synthetic glory, they recalled to Alloway's mind the decidedly un-modernist notion of 'an heraldic display'.[37] At Crosby's IUAC South Bank building in July 1961, Plumb exhibited with Bernard Cohen and Peter Stroud in the western precinct, with one of the largest modernist pictures created in London – *White Centre 4* (1961) . This was twenty-four feet long and eight feet high, 'taped' *in situ* onto Asbestolux boards by Plumb, 'reacting to the existing physical elements, in this case colour and the environment'.[38] Stroud spoke of his steel rod relief contribution to this courtyard in terms of environmental artwork that functioned publicly by 'moulding forms of splendour',[39] a phrase which rings with civic excess for Plumb as well, a momentary recuperation of fabulous historical colour from the most novel and recent of synthetic substances.

At the RBA Gallery 'Situation' show Gordon House showed two huge lozenge-shaped canvases (a format Plumb was to adopt over the next year), eight feet in length, generically called *Diagonal* (1960). In rooms of ambiguous coloured objects these vast kites appeared amongst the most startling: one hung resting its axial point on the floor, its companion floated up, ascending. These grave and gay paintings used stripes horizontally and vertically to give an optical flicker, a quality Alloway disparaged when he discovered it in Denny's *Baby is Three* (1960) next door. The precision and incisiveness of House's pictures reflected his allied talents as the most refined graphic designer of his generation. He had worked for ICI in pharmaceuticals and in their Plastic Division, and he had encountered the Swiss style of cool, logical typography and design through Geigy Heute, a school of design that sprang from the European inter-war period of rationalised modernity. Seizing on the crisp, spare elegance of the Helvetica and Universe typefaces and the purist opening up of large areas of white space on a page, House worked to revolutionise the graphic presentation of key London art galleries involved in contemporary art, particularly the Marlborough offshoot pioneered by David Gibbs, the Marlborough New London Gallery. House also designed cards and graphics for Kasmin's gallery which opened in April 1963. 'Situation', while avoiding any cohesive art-style, nevertheless was the first wholly *designed* twentieth-century English vanguard: House made sure that catalogue, notepaper and poster carried the same identity – a cool, clean, monochrome, and distinctively European image.

What House did for the graphic design of 'Situation' and the larger avant-garde, Robert Freeman accomplished in the realm of photographic presentation: more – in Plumb's words, 'Freeman was part of the group, like Gordon (House), but as a photographer he was more than just a documenter or portraitist ... he was like Stieglitz, he transmitted the new style.'[40] At

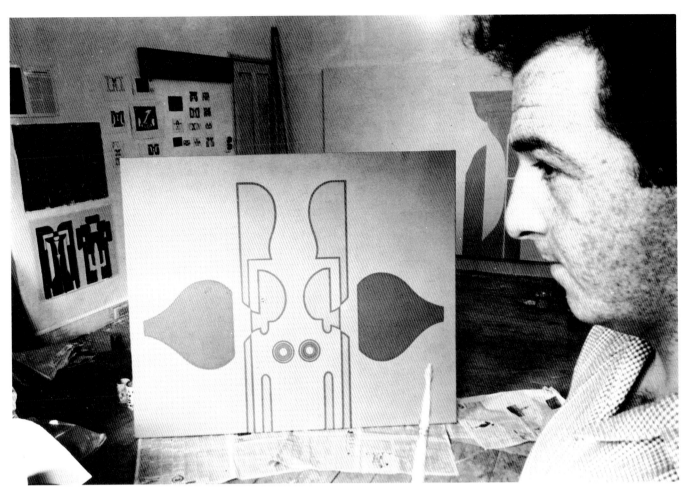

Robert Freeman,
Bernard Cohen in his studio,
1961

Robert Freeman,
Mark Vaux,
1961

one level it was routine – if inspired – documentation; it was Freeman's photographs of Caro's new works of 1960–61 that Alloway took to New York to Greenberg: 'Clem just flipped when he saw these!'[41] he told Denny later. But with his portraits of the 'Situation' artists for the Marlborough New London Gallery exhibition catalogue of August–September 1961, he altered all the co-ordinates for presenting painters and sculptors by using the 'Situation' sense of an enveloping, environmental space in his photographs. As he photographed them, the artists are proximate intruders into their own artefacts' space: Hoyland rises up in front of his painting as if in the configuration of 24 Hours, while Vaux is boxed in by his paintings. These studio scenes are shot with a wide angle lens, pulling a whole room into view with, invariably, the artist or a specimen picture drastically flattening the foreground. What Coleman called 'perceptual instability'[42] abounds in Freeman's catalogue portraits. The paintings lean casually in the studio/domestic environment, garden or pavement; off-duty, informal in their formality. After clearing the ground for new portrayals of painters, Freeman continued his career in the similarly shifting spaces of the pop music industry. These are intimate scenes of frontal yet unlocatable, stylish bodies. He turned in September 1963 to the upcoming Beatles: he photographed their heads in stark flat confrontation for *With the Beatles* (1963), and went on to collaborate with Dick Lester on the making of *Hard Day's Night* (1964) and *Help!* (1965): throughout the mid-Sixties the bodies of the Beatles were continually over-coded by the spaces and meanings that Freeman had encountered and shaped during his earlier 'Situation' period.

Robyn Denny,
Track 4, 1961
Oil on canvas, 183 x 183 cm
Artist's collection

Gordon House,
Diagonal, 1960
Casein on canvas, 239 cm high
Artist's collection

The first 'Situation' exhibition had the effect of showing the gathering of talented sculptors at St. Martin's that – in the words of Tim Scott – 'British painting was getting off the ground; this then led to a challenge by the sculptors'.[1] The 'challenge', when it came, arrived quickly and in the very areas that the painters had staked out – flat fields of colour; single, emblematic images; industrial materials; environmental scale and spectatorial confrontation.

Phillip King,
Rosebud, 1962
Plastic, 152 x 183 x 183 cm
Artist's collection

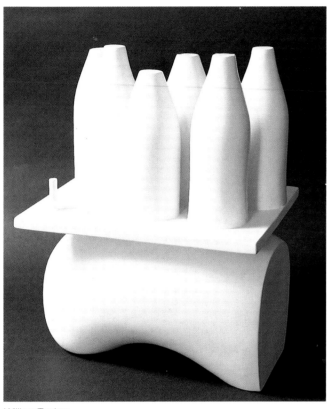

William Tucker,
Ceremonial, 1961–2
Plastic, 35 cm high
Private collection

Anthony Caro,
Capital, 1961
at IUAC, South Bank, 1961

A new spirit of contact and emulation grew up: for instance, Turnbull's enthusiasm for Caro, Smith's discussions with King, the friendship between John Hoyland and William Tucker, contacts that were evident through the number of 'Situation' painters – such as Bernard Cohen and Turnbull – who joined the sculpture 'crits' at St. Martin's. It was a crucial but sadly fragile moment that lasted only for the few years of 1960 to 1963 – 'one of the nice things,' Tim Scott pointed out, 'was the interaction ... then Pop came along'.[2] The sculptors – and particularly Tucker – argued a case for reclaiming the singularity of sculpture as 'thing', as a material object in the world. 'Unlike painting,' wrote the poet Christopher Salveson in the St. Martin's sculpture magazine *First 2*, 'there is no illusion about sculpture; it is materially assertive – it projects 3-D in a 3-D world',[3] although he admitted that the precedents for what the sculptors desired to make 'are probably in painting and poetry'.[4] The creative ambivalence which arose from this double-take would literally colour sculpture for the first part of the Sixties

It was Tucker who theorised that ambiguous 'thing' which might be sculpture by drawing upon Heidegger's philosophy and, at first in 1961, upon the existential meditations on history of Hannah Arendt. She had pictured a world of conditioned human existence filled with instrumental objects which in their utility had fixed identities rather than being an ambiguous 'heap of unrelated articles, a non-world ...'[5]; Tucker wished to assert the possibility of a new sculpture that, stripped of profane familiarity, partook of just such a liminal 'non-world, as yet unexplored between human beings and the world of recognisable, useful, conditioning things in which they live'.[6] Tucker's enigmatic *Ceremonial* (1961–2) from his first exhibition at the Grabowski Gallery in April 1962, took the banalities of milk bottles as social objects and instead cast their interior volume into just such a 'non-world' situation, reflexively, as milky white polyester 'things'.[7] This unclassified zone – a non-world – of essentially strange presences – had been stumbled on in Sartre's *La Nausée*, and the 'otherness' which dwelt on the earth had been a major pre-occupation of phenomenological thought. This position seems to have been central to Tucker, King and Scott by 1961–2 and was foundational to the St. Martin's sculpture which followed.

The neutral polyester and fibreglass skins of King, Tucker and Scott's sculptures stood somewhat apart in meaning from Caro's use of welded sheet metal, conduits and rolled steel joists. His attitude – the direct use of impersonal industrial materials – marked the shared common ground with them, but not his emphasis on the segmented process of assembling pre-formed metal units on a part-to-part basis. The spectator reading the formal linkages of girders connecting with angled plates became aware, as Gene Baro suggested, of 'a sequence of events that develops into the whole form'.[8] Along the low axii of *Midday* (1961) and *Early One Morning* (1962), a series of formal events occurred as if notated in time by the close-up maker and spectator, the remnant of gestural Action. There was also the element of disclosure of means (a self-reflexive protocol) in the 'overtly exposed bolts'[9] that held Caro's metal assemblies together and that Jasia Reichardt

Cover of
`Gazette`,
with Anthony
Caro interview,
1961

Gazette

Number 1 1961

Editors:
Lawrence Alloway
Gordon House
William Turnbull

Printed Litho. by the Graphis Press Limited
Designed by Gordon House

Interview with Anthony Caro
by Lawrence Alloway

Q. Did your visit to America in Autumn 1959 affect your style-change?

A. Before I went to America my work was changing. In my late figures the image was beginning to disappear. I felt that the figure was getting in the way. Also I think I was enjoying the clay too much — it was beginning to take charge.

America was certainly the catalyst in the change. For one think I realised that I had nothing to lose by throwing out History —here we are all steeped in it anyway. There's a fine-art quality about European art even when it's made from junk. America made me see that there are no barriers and no regulations — they simply aren't bound to traditional or

conventional solutions in their art or in anything else, behaviour, roads or anything. There's a tremendous freedom in knowing that your only limitations in a sculpture or painting whether it carries its intention or not, not whether it's Art.

Q. Why did you change from plaster to welding in 1960?

A. I wanted to get away from the old sort of work associated with plaster and clay, and I thought the best way was to change my habits. I did try to do a non-figurative sculpture in plaster, but it got lost somewhere between being a body and and an abstract.

Q. What are your new materials?

A. Different sized sheets and sections. In the scrap yards at the docks you can choose from a big variety of almost new simple elements like R.S.J.'s and channels. I'm not interested in how the elements would have been used. But when I'm working I don't like to give the elements too much personal processing either.

At the beginning I used to get bits that were nice shapes, but now I just want materials. I shaped my first metal works, too, but discarded them. It's the primary fact of the unit that I like. It's the assembling of the whole forms, not the modifying of single bits that I want.

Q. Are your new sculptures aimed for one site or many?

A. Anywhere. Except that I prefer to think of my sculptures indoors. Indoors they should expand into a space. Outside when you can get back to look at them from a distance the grip of the sculpture is diffused. I know that when I work on a sculpture out of doors I have room to stand back and that only encourages me to worry about the balance and that sort of thing; and that invariably ruins it. Working indoors in a restricted space and close up all the time my decisions don't bear on the thing's all round appearance. They're not compositional decisions.

Anyway I'm not interested in monuments. I'm fed up with objects on pedestals. I'd like to break down the graspability of sculpture. Sculpture is terifically tangible, but a painting however concrete is partly in the realm of illusion. That's one reason why I like Noland's so-called targets so much more than Johns'. Sculpture becomes more intangible when you can't see it at all easily or fully.

Q. In a sense then your new work is a development rather than a DENIAL OF YOUR figurative work. Your figures seemed as real as rocks and yet hard to focus on in detail. They were substantial and illusive. For all the change in your art, these qualities are still present, don't you think?

A. Yes.

Sculpture 5 1960
Steel painted yellow 7' 10'' high x 3' 2'' wide x 12' long

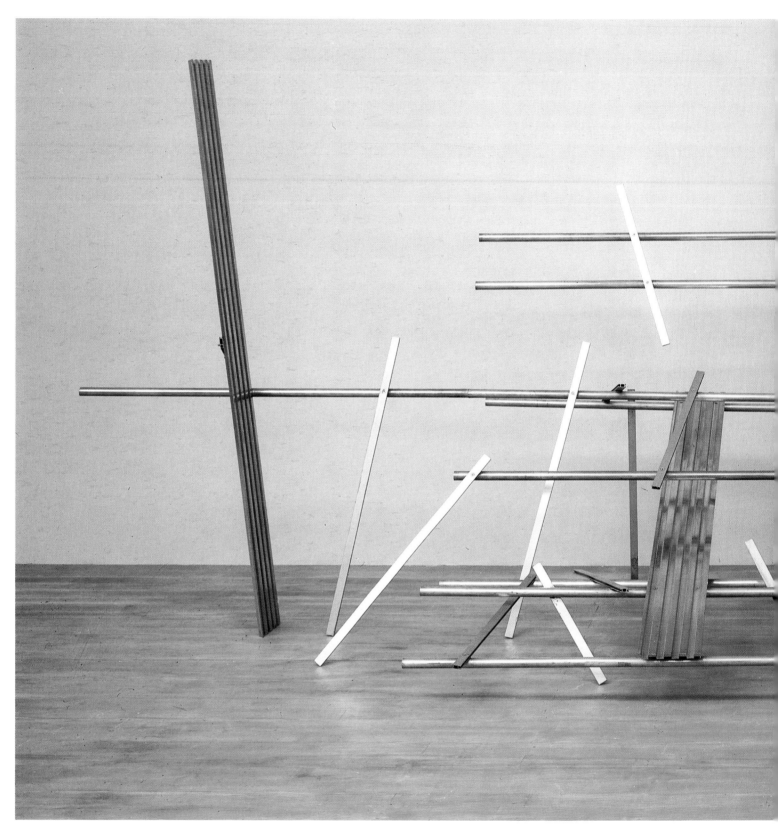

Anthony Caro,
Hopscotch, 1962
Aluminium, 250 x 475 x 213 cm
Artist's collection

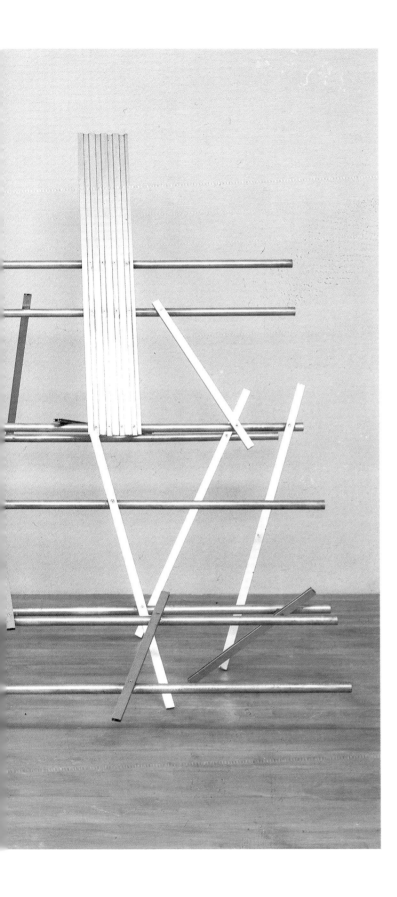

noted as marking Caro off from other sheet-metal sculpture welders like Brian Wall and Robert Adams. Declarations of means of artifice became part of the rhetoric of the renewed modernism of London in the early Sixties. It was entwined with the display of medium, an opening of the codes of fabrication, comparable with the flaunting of TV cameras, microphone booms and the presence of studio floor technicians in shot, during broadcasts of the TV satire programme, *That Was The Week That Was*, late in 1962. Kenneth Noland's display of the means of fabricating his stained colour abstracts had been inspirational to Caro at the end of 1959, sustaining his own moment of transformation. Colour overtook what Caro, in his 1961 interview with Alloway, called the 'tangibility',[10] of sculpture, camouflaging its 'graspability'[11]: a countervailing force to the admission of its own facticity.

The sanction to enable Caro to dismantle a certain tradition of modernist sculpture – particularly of the organic and pastoralist variety – came from American culture: here was a pragmatism that looked askance at history and authority. Clement Greenberg's affirmations of the need for innovative authenticity – of absolute authorial commitment to intention and responsibility for the form and style of the art-work, were important. This was summed up in Greenberg's pithy, withering comment on an English artist: 'He doesn't want to be good; he wants to be right'.[12] That is, the artist wanted to cleave to the established havens of artistic authority, rather than attempt the existential leap to make values. 'America certainly was the catalyst',[13] Caro affirmed to Alloway; just as Alloway had used the urban and technical romance of US culture as a blunt weapon against the English art establishment, America was to appear across the board as similar corrective to English conservatism of habit. For the Cambridge satirists – the contemporaries of Robert Freeman – at London's Establishment Club, as well as for artists like Bruce Lacey, such a quest for authenticity of voice and heroic dissent against British norms of institutional and civil behaviour came in the guise of the American comedian Lenny Bruce. It was the fantasy ideal of a freer mental climate, contrasting to that in moribund Britain, that drew not just Caro, but a number of London artists who would visit or base themselves in the US: Turnbull in 1957, Harold Cohen and Richard Smith in 1959, Hockney in 1961, Laing and Phillips in 1964, and so on.

'The results are nearer to abstract painting in three dimensions than to anything normally thought of as sculptural'[14] ran the testimony of David Thompson on Caro's pictorialist break with sculptural tradition. To Greenberg, *Early One Morning* was rooted in the collage tradition; to Bridget Riley, on first appearance, it resembled 'a painting that had been pulled out of its frame'.[15] *Early One Morning* seemed to contain an allegorical easel at one end with the large rectangle standing in as a red monochrome canvas; a sign of painting. While colour might disembody the sculpture's perceived weighty mass, according to the developing phenomenological criticism of Michael Fried, this sculpture embodied a sense of human livedness. The body is seen by Fried as the prime referent: '.. the central concept for understanding Caro's art is that of the body ...' From his interest in Maurice Merleau-Ponty's thought,

Bob Whittaker,
Anthony Caro's **Prairie** at Kasmin Ltd.,
1967

Fried, at the time of Caro's first major exhibition at the Whitechapel in September and October 1963, made the audacious move of imagining Caro's sculptures as analogues of human movement and gesture. 'For all their abstraction', he wrote, 'one can imagine a gifted dancer dancing Caro's sculpture'.[16]

With this Fried moved beyond that matrix of ideas involving Action painting as an arena for the body, and ventured towards the new discourse around the language of the freed body, a discourse that came into circulation in that more liberal moment of the Sixties, a body expressive of open exuberance after the angst of the Forties and Fifties: the privileging of a body defying gravity and the previous limitations of the tragic view. As the Sixties ended and a certain sense of optimism connected with the body also waned, the English critic Charles Harrison insisted on removing Fried's image of Caro's incorporateness of body and sculpture, by curtailing the somatic register to one of mental sensations alone: 'There are no references to the body; only to the open mind within the body'.[17] For Phillip King the period of the early and middle Sixties was a utopian one of 'unlimited human possibilities'.[18] It could be argued that – in common with other St. Martin's sculptors – many of King's sculptures asserted a morphology of rising, potentially ecstatic, forms that could be associated with the 'dance' that was evident in Caro's *Hopscotch* and *Month of May* (both 1962). The paradoxes of such uplifting, dematerialised 'lightness' was a trope in the new sculpture which was perceptively monitered by the critic Jasia Reichardt in 1965. With David Annesley's *Swing Low* (1964) a ribbon of striped green and blue ran wavily through two stacked, open, yellow packages. The referent for the pack forms was cardboard, light and flimsy; for Reichardt this is witty, 'contrived ... whereas in fact the material is steel'.[19] Tucker's *Meru* sculptures of 1964 'enclose space like bridges'[20] and an abstract iconography of ascension marks these and *Anabasis I* and *II* (1964), which rise by ever diminishing steps from solid 3-D single images into a transparent, schematic reminder of that shape. As sculpture stripped painting's assets, Richard Smith, who was also teaching at St. Martin's in the painting department between 1961 and 1963, tried to appropriate characteristics of sculpture for painting, particularly with his exhibition at Kasmin's in November 1963. As the Sixties continued, his works negotiated this common iconography of weightlessness. In 1966, with drawing projects for painting/sculptures, he returned to that festive 'marquee' sensibility that Alloway had attributed to him in 1962. In the new pastoral of the parklands of 'Swinging London' Smith proposed to erect high striped canvases supported by masts and ropes and tent pegs; banners again, in the 'Situation' mode: 'everything that is gay and airy'.[21]

Such physically ascensional images which characterised the new sculpture were contingent upon colour and its connotational and erotic possibilities. Smith had written a short essay, 'That Pink',[22] almost in the style – yet independent – of Roland Barthes' *Mythologies* articles, discussing Irving Penn's colour photography. Richard Hamilton was to take up some of Smith's ideas in his text 'Urbane Image' in 1963, and in his

Gordon House,
Invitation card to
The 118 Show, Kas
1963

'For all their
abstraction ...
one can imagine
a gifted dancer
dancing Caro's
sculpture'

Anthony Caro,
Month of May, 1962
Painted steel and aluminium,
280 x 305 x 360 cm
Artist's collection

Gerald Nason,
Princess Margaret, photomontage (suppressed), *ARK magazine*,
1963

by larger systems of technical forces. In his painting, *Panoply* (1964) Laing clothed his astronauts, schematising them as iconic, head-on – like his 'continental' film stars – and he decorated the painting with insignias; the badge of NASA and vernacular 'hot-rod' flames. The result is akin to Alloway's description of 'Situation' paintings as banners – except Laing literalises the heraldic aspect of the astronauts into a techno-chivalric pennant. Following William Green's enthusiasm for American 'dragster' cars, Laing had himself photographed in London for the promotion of his New York exhibition, in front of Horse Guards Parade in Whitehall, seated in an imported 'hot-rod'. This figured a clash of cultural signs, those of tradition and a transgressive, US-style, modernity. With Reyner Banham, Laing put together an exhaustive survey of dragster heraldry following the exhibition of customised hot-rods which he held at Richard Feigen's in the autumn of 1964.[14] This cult of the American racer was already in place at the end of the Fifties, joining the memorial cult around James Dean to which Geoff Reeve contributed with his *Maquette for a Monument to James Dean* (1960). In Tony Messenger's stupendous painting of Dean's wrecked Porsche, *30th September 1955,* shown at the 'Young Contemporaries' exhibition of 1958, Richard Diebenkorn blends with John Bratby in vehemence. It rivalled, from a position of impastoed Realism, the fading history painting epic of John Minton's treatment of the same iconography, *The Death of James Dean* (1957).

After this high tragic apotheosis of modern masculinity in the wave of memorial images to Dean (and to Albert Camus), the other route to represent the male body was through comedy. For Bruce Lacey his two elected heroes were 'John Minton for his enthusiasm and Lenny Bruce for his morality'.[15] Like Lenny Bruce's scabrous comedy routines, Lacey's art was predicated on a loathing for the consumer era of 'Never had it so good'[16] and a desire 'to shock people out of their complacency'.[17] In the late Fifties Lacey opened an absurdist sub-genre of black domestic comedy with his manic uses of electrical assemblages. He worked for ITV, in its early years in the mid-Fifties, with Peter Sellers on *A Show Called Fred*, and the recently arrived Canadian director, Dick Lester. In his self-devised role as 'The Preservation Man', Lacey assembled large quantities of National Health and H.M. Forces surpluses, which were the detritus of the Cold War Welfare State – scores of spare limbs, jettisonable fuel pods for RAF jet fighters, eye-patches, Meteorological Office balloons ... all surplus, and all to be recycled in his comedy performances. For his collaborations with his old RCA friends, the comedy-music group The Alberts, Lacey gathered from the Portobello Road, from Lawrence Corner and other London army surplus shops, a vast collection of old military uniforms, to be worn during their Establishment Club, 'Evening of British Rubbish' performances. This was a probable point of origin, with Peter Blake, of the late Sixties militaria fashion in alternative culture, that uneasy coalition of satire, nostalgia and de-constructive dress codes. Like Latham's brief appearance at Kasmin Ltd. in 1963, Lacey was temporarily brought into the circuits of high modernist art consumption by the Marlborough New London Gallery who showed his assemblages in January 1965. His eventist cre-

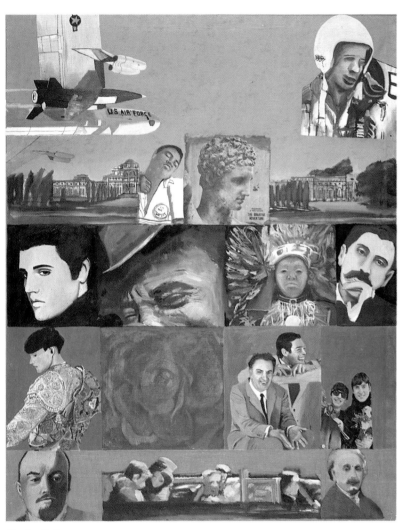

Pauline Boty,
It's A Man's World I, 1963
Oil on canvas with collage, 91 x 122 cm
Private collection

dentials were impeccable; he had, for instance, assisted Jean Tinguely at the latter's ICA performance in 1959, with a writing machine that spewed its script into Dover Street. Then, in the early Sixties, Lacey had begun building Dexion scaffoldings for his electronically operated comic robots, complete with their Welfare State prosthetics. His Keinholz-esque kinetic sculpture, *The Womaniser* (1965-6) dates from the time of his show at the Marlborough; part 'Junk'-sculpture and part motorised inflatable. This machine grotesquerie also keyed with other elements in contemporary taste: for example, N. F. Simpson's absurdist Royal Court play, *One Way Pendulum* (1959) in which William Green's friend, Roddy Maude Roxby, played the role of a crazed suburban youth who collects weighing machines and teaches them how to sing.

Lacey's junk-dramas suggested the associations of contemporary 'sick humour'. This was the Lenny Bruce-ian theatre of cathartic buffoonery: but when Richard Hamilton assembled some favourite chosen objects for a mute performance in the spring of 1963, his comic genre was nearer the cool, sardonic wit of other American comics such as Bob Newhart. In a photographed tableau which he later titled 'Self Portrait' for the cover of *Living Arts*, to complement his essay 'Urbane Image',[18] Hamilton asserted his absolute contemporaneity and Americanophilia through a display of pristine products, gathered as props. For these he gave credits at the close of his text: 'Producer Richard Hamilton/Photographer Robert Freeman/Stylist Betsy Schermer ...'[19] as well as for the individual suppliers. It was a comic tableau, a conglomerate 'kit' for the contingencies of urban and inter-stellar living (the NASA Mercury capsule was secured by Betsy Schermer from Ken Adam's James Bond set at Shepperton). These were arguably more prosthetics (not Lacey's fly-blown fetishes), extensions of Hamilton in the role Alloway assigned to him of 'the knowing consumer'. There was a super-portable combined radio and record player, the Wondergram (supplied by Sherbourne TV Services), playing an LP by the US pop singer, Gene Vincent (then residing in Britain) and his backing group, the Bluecaps: there was a Hoover Constellation vacuum cleaner, its nozzle snaking like the sperm's tail from Hamilton's earlier self-portraying forays into biological imagery in the earlier Fifties.[20] Like Marcel Duchamp's *Bride Stripped Bare*, Hamilton had composed a comedy of sexual division and distance – the model separated, on the boot of the '63 Thunderbird and on the back page of the magazine cover, from Hamilton's front cover US football player, girded in an outfit kindly lent by the American High School in London. This US commodity cornucopia was displayed on a pink fabric ground; Dick Smith, enthusiast for 'That Pink', was present that day, as was Gordon House and Robert Freeman, who photographed the entire scene. Hamilton's essentially American self-fashioning was burlesque but elegant. When accused of 'knocking America'[21] by the US Cultural Attache, Stefan Munsing, he insisted that he was not producing satirical paintings of hybrid astronauts-cum-football players. On the contrary Hamilton was arriving consciously at a celebration of Americana by what Ezra Pound had called the 'modern mythic method'. Where Kitaj and Boty had de-stabilised and dismantled a noble classical past as a template for

Photograph of Pauline Boty and
Derek Boshier

the present, Hamilton – inspired by Joyce's correlation, in **143**
Ulysses, of classical narrative and a profane present – wished
instead to maintain it. 'We live' he wrote in the text 'Urbane
Image', 'in an era in which the epic is realised...'[22]

The promotional fashioning of David Hockney was one of the
key events of the early Sixties. His body very rapidly became
synonymous with the body of fame and then became disem-
bodied as a media legend. In one of his very first published
profiles, in February 1962 in *Queen*, he appeared in a blurred
portrait photograph and was described as an 'emergent blur'.[23]
This 'blur' signified the velocity of his perceived success: he
was elevated by word of mouth, a murmur spoken in the litany
of success which his promotion in the new London media fur-
thered. His was a passage to fame through the advent of
certain mechanisms of celebrity that were now available after
the renovation of the 'glossies' – particularly *Queen* under
Jocelyn Stevens, and *Town* under the art direction of Tom
Wolsey. From 1960–1 these magazines geared themselves to
a new audience of affluent knowing consumers, 'pacey' individuals who were aware of 'trends'. Hockney is the great

Pauline Boty,
It's A Man's World II, 1963-65
Oil on canvas, 122 x 122 cm
Private collection

Pauline Boty,
The Only Blonde in the World, 1964
Oil on canvas, 122 x 152 cm
Private collection

Peter Blake,
Girlie Door, 1959
Collage and oil on wood,
122 x 58 cm
Joe Tilson

Richard Smith,
MM, 1959
Oil on canvas, 91 x 91 cm
Private collection

Richard Hamilton,
My Marilyn, 1965
Screen print, 51 x 63 cm
Private collection

exemplar, before the Beatles, of mastery over this new publicity machinery by means of ironising the reporting of fame. As the Hockney narrative gathered strength through 1962 and into 1963, authentic provincial traits – 'He retains his Yorkshire accent and tends to rub his chest while talking'[24] – were played off against camp signifiers of lack of depth and extreme artifice. The metropolitan culture was deeply engaged with the fantasy of 'Northern-ness' from 1960 and the arrival of actors Tom Courtney, Albert Finney and other demonstrable 'northerners', combined with the establishment of the 'North' as a mythical site in drama, cinema and TV. Hockney, therefore, was 'emergent' at and contributes to this moment. His amiability was qualified by an Orton-esque weirdness: 'It was a bright afternoon, but before we could talk Hockney had to draw all the curtains. 'I have very inquisitive neighbours', he said'.[25] By the end of 1963, and his first Kasmin exhibition he was elevated to the status of male idol, the fascinating star in his own right. He had been the 'sincere fan' of Cliff Richard, now he also had become a star: 'Will success spoil David Hockney?' asked *The Tatler*, in December 1963,[26] in citation of the Hollywood film, *Will Success Spoil Rock Hunter?*. William Green had been the only comparably publicised painter-hero of the period and by 1962 he was withdrawing from the limelight, beginning his thirty-year exile from media attention. 'It is the artists who are continually exploited and usually wrecked through loss of time and vulgarisation of their image',[27] warned Bryan Robertson, reflecting on the new processes of media celebration of the artist. As 1963 ended he described Hockney as an endlessly multiplied 'special effect' in a repetitive hall of promotional mirrors. 'At the preview party for the prints show, for instance, Mr Hockney's prints were around the walls, Mr Hockney and his friends were amongst the guests, and on a blank wall at one end of the gallery a TV screen projected an additional image of Mr Hockney being interviewed on a popular TV programme'.[28]

From an image of embrace, of felicity and union - The Three Graces by Canova – Kitaj wreaks dislocations and produces new meanings.

R B Kitaj,
An Early Europe, 1964
Oil on canvas, 152 x 213 cm
Private collection

Allen Jones,
La Sheer, 1968
Oil on canvas, 183 x 152 cm with steps,
46 x 152 cm
Private collection

Robert Freeman,
Promotional sheet for
Billy Apple Exhibition,
Gallery One, 1963

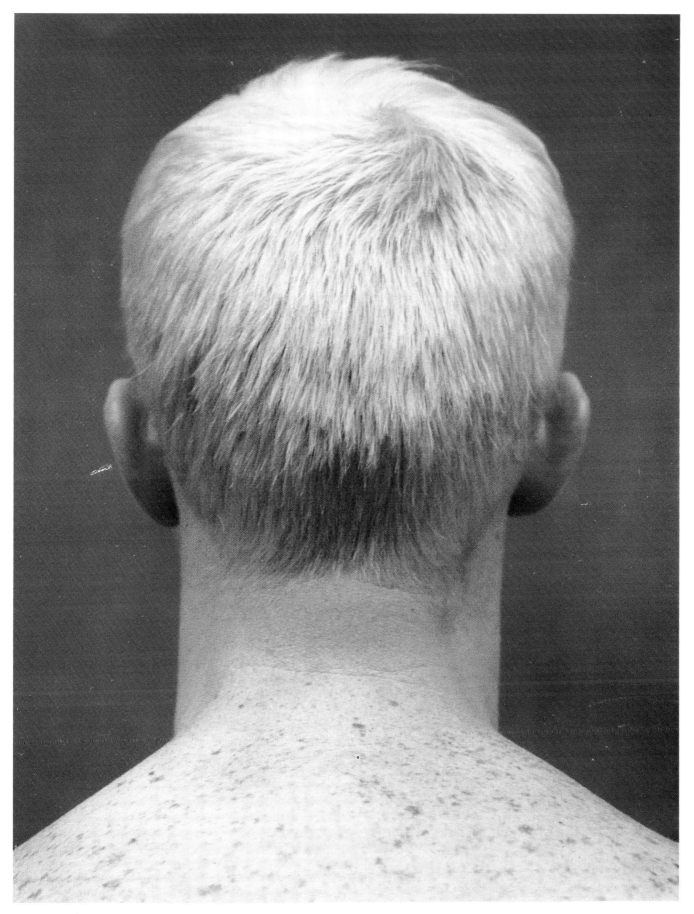

Apple sees red

Live Stills by Billy Apple on show at Gallery One, 16 North Audley Street, Grosvenor Square, London, W.1.
HYDe Park 5880. April 1st. to 20th., Mondays to Fridays 10 a.m. to 6 p.m. and Saturdays 11 a.m. until 1 p.m.

Photograph of Gerald Laing painting **Brigitte Bardot**, 1963

'We don't know
Brigitte Bardot – we
know her through the
newspaper image.'

Gerald Laing,
Brigitte Bardot,
1963
Oil on canvas,
152 x 122 cm
Private collection

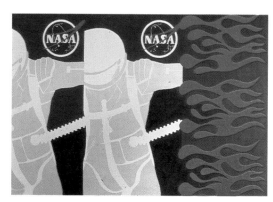

Gerald Laing,
Panoply, 1964
Oil on canvas, 122 x 168 cm
Artist's collection

Raymond Hawkey,
4-3-2-1-zero, 1961
Graphic design from
The Daily Express

Derek Boshier,
Rethinking, Re-Entry, 1962
Oil on canvas, 183 x 183 cm
Private collection

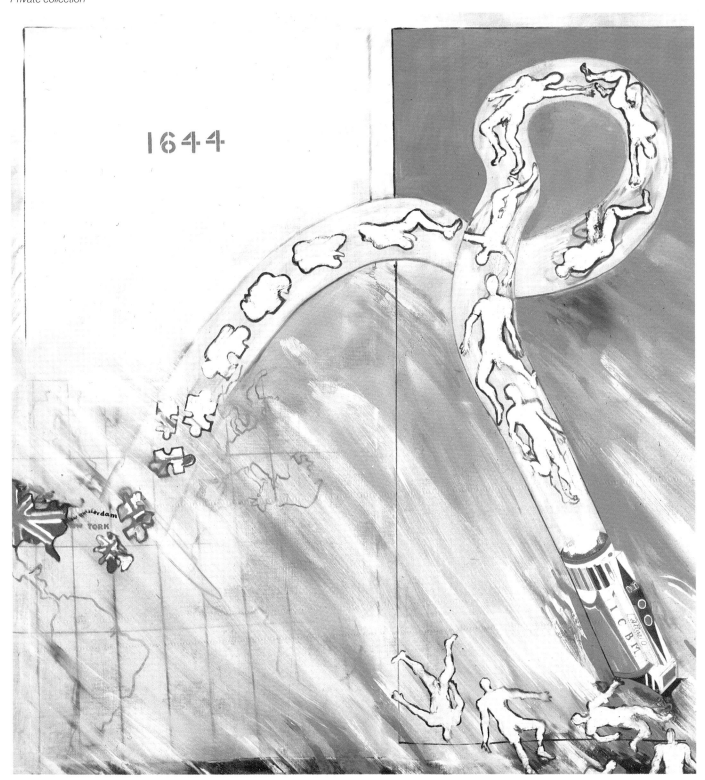

Tony Messenger,
30th September 1955, 1958
Oil on panel, 122 x 244 cm
Private collection

Gerald Laing in a Dragster,
Promotional sheet for Richard Feigen Gallery Exhibition,
1964

Geoff Reeve,
**Maquette for a monument
to James Dean,**
1960

John Minton,
Composition, Death of James Dean, 1957
Oil on canvas, 122 x 183 cm
Tate Gallery, London

the
first exhibition of
automata and
humanoids
by Bruce Lacey
at
Gallery One
16 North Audley
Street
Grosvenor Square
London WI
HYDe Park 5880
June 1963

Bruce Lacey, Gallery One catalogue cover,
1963

In the late Fifties
Lacey opened
an absurdist
sub-genre of black
domestic comedy
with his manic
uses of electrical
assemblages.

Bruce Lacey,
The Womaniser, 1965-66
Wood, plastic and rubber
152 x 275 x 91 cm
Artist's collection

Overleaf:
Robert Freeman,
preparation of
Self Portrait
(Richard Hamilton),
1963

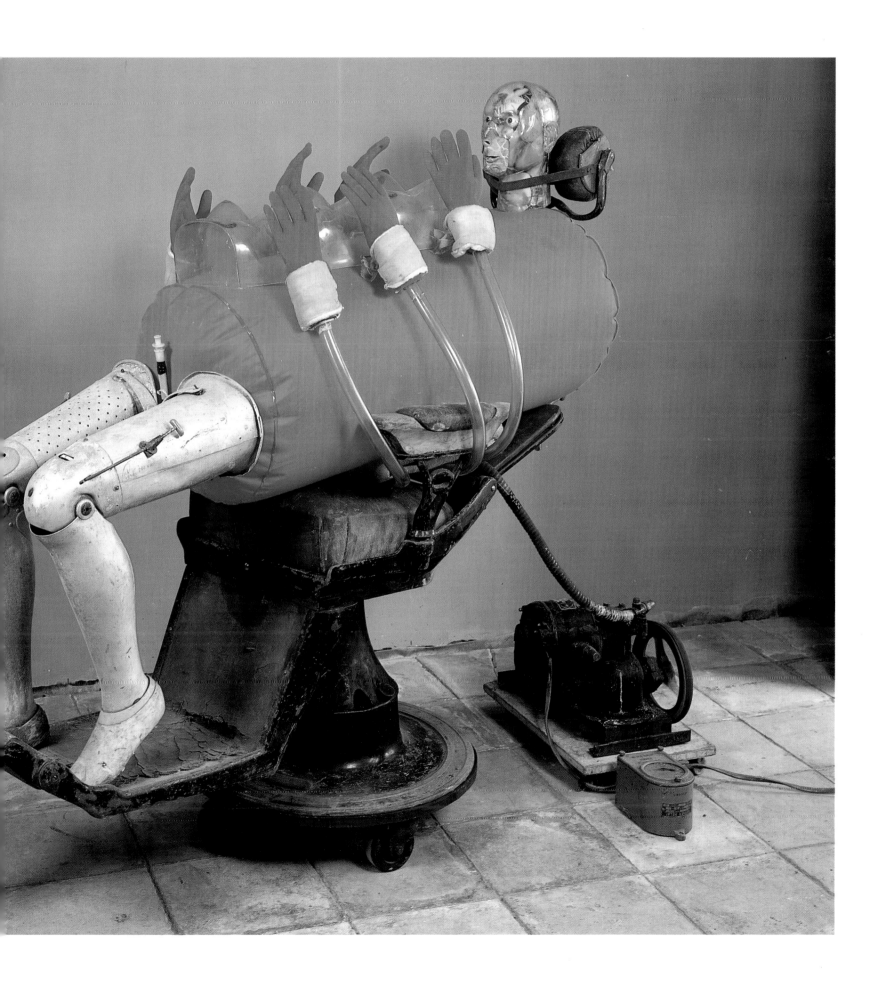

162

Geoff Reeve,
Photograph of David Hockney and Derek Boshier,
1961-62

Hockney is the great exemplar, before the Beatles, of mastery over this new publicity machinery by means of ironising the reporting of fame.

Gerald Laing,
London Artists in Paris,
1963
From left to right:
Terry Stewart,
Francis Morland;
(foreground group)
Marquis of Dufferin and Ava,
Kasmin, David Hockney;
(at the back)
Norbert Lynton,
2 British Council officers,
Joe Tilson,
Peter Blake,
Allen Jones (with umbrella),
Mr and Mrs Gerald Laing,
Derek Boshier,
Peter Phillips,
Mark Berger

The dematerialisation of the art object was variously imagined by artists at the end of the Sixties: dematerialised, that is, in terms of its customary contextual institutions and its relocation in pockets of an increasingly politicised world. Reyner Banham, speaking in 1967, presented a milleniary prospect: he foresaw the twilight of an isolated, contemplative art which might only persist as 'a kind of licensed fetishism'[1]: an art which would be superannuated by the

Richard Hollis,
At Hornsey ..., 1968
Poster
Artist's collection

evolution of forms generated by 'the more open kind of democracy which a lot of people are fighting for'.[2] It is notable that acknowledgement of Roy Ascott's seminal role in this process in England was made by the use of a statement by Roy Ascott as the motto at the beginning of Lucy Lippard's first, compendious study of conceptual art, *Six Years, the Dematerialisation of the Art Object* (1973). At the end of the decade such a 'dematerialisation' of art was posited by, among others, Brisley, the Event Structures Research Group, John Latham's associated Artists Placement Group and by the coalescing Art and Language circle.

The participatory arena which Banham described was fast becoming a matter of polarised political contest. In July 1966 the Labour government of Harold Wilson was, in his own words, 'blown off course' by the worsening economic position. The resulting credit squeeze was, in part, responsible for a contraction in the London art world and the closure of galleries.[3] But, on a wider scale than this, political dissent, fuelled by the Vietnam war and the rise of international student protest, became more marked than at any time since the early Sixties and the heyday of CND. The Destruction in Art Symposium (DIAS), organised by Gustav Metzger in September 1966, took as its background Metzger's already established apocalyptic diagnosis of culture and politics. As he wrote during the preparations for a politicised 'Artists' Council' in London in the summer of 1969: 'We are in a society whose basis is the production, the selling and maintaining of systems of mass-murder. It is against this reality that other forms of social activity must be placed'.[4] Self-organisation and groups of 'artists' democracies' modelled on political cells were spawned in the year after the most disruptive challenge to the institutions of British art education, the occupations of colleges in the spring and summer of 1968 at Hornsey, Guildford and elsewhere, in furious emulation of the larger political upheavals on the continent.

The polarisation which ensued redirected Stuart Brisley's art. Teaching at Hornsey at the time, he felt that 'the events of '68 had a galvanising effect on me. It illuminated the direction I had been fumbling for...'[5] This direction was towards a performance art of the most visceral kind 'using one's own body as vehicle and image',[6] thus renewing his contract with an actionism which he had practised in 1960, but was now re-focused on the body itself, rather than on its painted traces. A few months before DIAS, Brisley had art-directed a photo session, with Robert Whittaker, for the promotion of the Beatles' single *Paperback Writer*. This involved the destruction (by the Beatles) of a set made from polystyrene and mirror-plastic sheeting. Brisley extended his collaborations with Bill Culbert, intervening drastically at a Tate Gallery event of Cesar's 'pourings' in March 1968.[7] But from the second half of 1968, after the watershed of the Hornsey occupation, he produced performances in public places in London – *Ritual Murder* at Hyde Park and *Swinging London* at Madame Tussaud's. A Sadian theme of the stark release of a subjectivity previously constrained by social and institutional organisations, colours these pieces of 1968–70. In contrast to the jubilatory performances celebrating the body in Mark Boyle's work, Brisley presented responses to social control in violent forms. It was the moment of the impact of Mary

Cover of **Black Dwarf**,
1 June 1968

Douglas' book, *Purity and Danger* (1966) which examined the rule-bound, anthropological situations of contamination and the maintenance of the 'proper person' and their body. In performances such as *Tower with Living Person* (at the important 'Environments Reversal' events at the Camden Arts Centre in June, 1969) and *Celebration for Institutional Consumption* (1970), Brisley explored what Julia Kristeva would call 'abjection': that vindication of excluded behaviour and matter,[8] the mess of life.

The pathos of the body, in Brisley's performances, arose from its unequal place in systems of social control. Stephan Willats shared part of this cultural premise of a bounded, culturalised world of predictable behaviour, but he wished to scrutinise these norms rather than expressionistically refuse them. With *Man from the 21st Century* (1969–70), Willats juxtaposed investigations into the dimensions of social choice and control in two areas of Nottingham: a typical Victorian terraced, working-class area, Hyson Green, the fading location of an industrial and artisanal culture, alongside a suburban middle-class housing development – Bramcote. It was an environmental project that tried to re-engage with documentarist and social survey techniques of information- and opinion-gathering in order to gauge the residents' habits and preferences. Not for the first time in this period did British avant-garde art annex the device of the questionnaire to try to model a public in all its diversity. To obtain a better access to these communities Willats – and his students from Trent Polytechnic – humorously presented the project as a promotional phenomenon, a mock advertising-campaign stunt. A 'Man from the 21st Century', a futurist figure in a silver jumpsuit, arrived in the neighbourhood (in an adapted Morris Minor as his time machine!) to ask residents to match their preferences to choices from photomontage charts of different ideal women, men, clothing, household objects and Bernstein-ian pictographs – 'basic codes'. Willats saw in the density of information elicited (which was relayed back to the respondents) a way to extend his programme of encouraging the emancipation of participant observers. With his light boxes it had been individuals who had become aware of the ordering they gave to phenomena – now Willats was extending this to entire communities. 'The artist,' he wrote at the time, 'by getting the audience to examine their social environment in a way that is not determined by the rules or routines for it, [could] perhaps find a way for people ... [to] control their own formation of needs and belief structure'.[9]

Willats had dealt with the everyday street environment – which Mark Boyle was proving, with his 'Presentations', to be extraordinary, a place of epiphanies. Other artists sought to re-clothe the spectators and participants who came to their constructed environments in visionary surroundings. In 1967, Banham had looked to the burgeoning sector of transparent plastic 'inflatables' to restore an almost pre-lapsarian community to those inside the plastic skins, and then to extend that utopia to the larger environment. Barriers were to be dissolved in 'this situation of the multiple input and free-form interaction with people and things around us'.[10] 'Other' utopian spaces seemed, to the techno-optimists, to be equally within reach. In the 'Underground' magazine, *Oz*, the following probability was

Derek Boshier,
Sex War Sex Cars Sex,
c.1967

Shape Chart

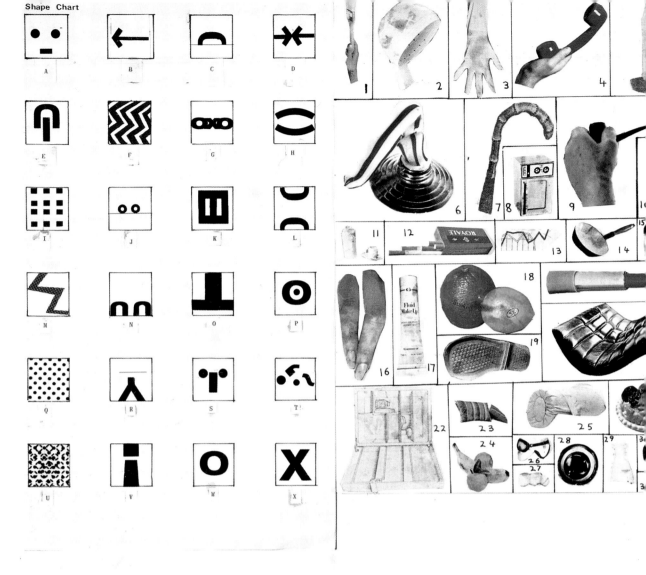

Face Chart

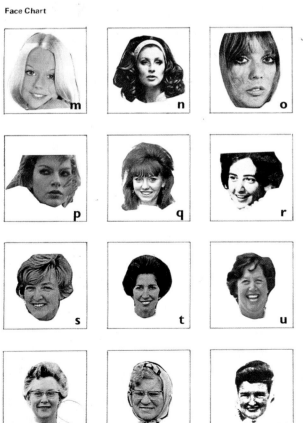

Clothes Chart

Stephen Willats,
The Man from the 21st Century, 1969-70
Letraset and collage, 33 x 20 cm each
Artist's collection

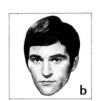

lothes Chart

sketched in the summer of 1967: 'All the indications are that we **193** are heading into an era when total environments will be commonplace – film as a moving tapestry on four walls and ceiling; strobe lights and coloured spots strategically placed ...'[11] The pneumatic inflatable structures of Jeff Shaw and Graham Stevens went further than this still fundamentally fixed – if psychedelic – interior space, to the dematerialised, free-form structure of the kind that Banham advocated. As with kinetic art, some influence came from France, with the 'Utopie' group which put on the 'Structures Gonflables' exhibition in Paris in May 1967.[12] A self- regulating 'peaceable kingdom' of play was promised from this new field of 'Pneumatics'. Peter Hobbs had a fantasy of such structures as early as 1958; they related to the benign, Kleinian image of claustral interiors that Ehrenzwieg had detected in his work. Such uterine spaces began to feature in photographic representations of inflatables, where bodies were packed joyfully together, in ideal images of masses of children seen through transparent membranes. It was here, in this imaginary space of 'Pneumatics', that the Sixties 'free body' found its final apotheosis. Tumbling, disorientated, buoyed up against gravity, discovering a second, sculptural skin, it was a condensation of all those prior images of leaping, parachuting, dancing and playing. The inflatables, first appearing in the larger public spaces of festivals, soon moved to more compact places: one of Graham Stevens' *Airmobiles* was located in the black Metro Community Club in Notting Hill by 1969–70. The miraculous – since participants could literally walk on water with Stevens' *Transmobile* – was combined with the democratic imperative of 'the personal being the political' (an insistent Women's Liberation slogan in 1969). At this moment of growing crisis in British social and political life, 'Pneumatics' were, in Graham Stevens' words, 'a tool for decreasing social barriers and increasing social contact and bodily awareness ... not exclusive of race, class, age group'.[13]

The metaphor of a pliable system was incarnated in SPACE, (Space Provision, Artistic, Cultural and Educational) the ambitious project which transformed St Katherine's Docks in early 1969. SPACE was devised by Bridget Riley and Peter Sedgley, with a co-operative of artists who joined them. From their original conception, at the end of 1967, the target was to find and refurbish a large studio space for artists among the now-derelict spaces and institutions of the nineteenth-century heart of empire. There was the old Marshalsea Prison in Southwark, a site that failed for SPACE: there was also the complex of warehouse buildings at St. Katherine's Docks, which Sedgley 'discovered', in May 1968. These vast London spaces lay empty because of structural change – both economic and social – which SPACE perceptively recognised as post-industrial opportunities. Sedgley told the *Daily Mirror*, 'Studio space is very difficult for artists to find in London'.[14] But with canny lobbying around the Arts Council and Establishment by Riley and Sedgley, the Greater London Council eventually leased the sixty thousand square feet of St Katherine's to SPACE for a limited time, before its re-development into the marina site, for a peppercorn rent. SPACE was another example of the expanding ideology of self-organisation within the avant-garde; it was manifest, in Sedgley's belief, that 'if all else failed the artist should

Jeff Shaw and Graham Stevens,
Inflatable Structure, St Katherine's Dock,
1969

The aim of hollowing out Victorian space to make in its stead a modernist, utopian one was also shared by the St Martin's sculptors, Maurice Agis and Peter Jones. They transformed a Fulham Road basement – an old carpenter's shop – into 'Space Place' in 1964. Like Archigram, Agis and Jones wanted to reconstitute an ideal civic space: 'The existing urban environment is (a) total accident – the result of incompetence by irresponsible idiots'.[16] Into this arbitrary corner of London, Agis and Jones established 'Space Place' as a thirty-five feet by twenty feet total environment of colour planes and painted metal rods: the Victorian milieu became the sort of coloured envelope which Alloway had hopefully imagined 'Situation' might be. But added to it was that strongly liberatory ethic that had developed in the late Sixties; Agis and Jones referred to 'this colour constructed area [where] a person does not need pre-conceived ideas to enjoy and experience it completely, its purpose is to liberate the senses ... a place for people to be participant, spectator and performer at the same time'.[17] The body, according to Agis and Jones, was restored in these coloured utopian spaces and when 'Space Place' was further developed at MOMA, Oxford in an installation in December 1966 it was utilised for performances by Yoko Ono and her dancers. 'Space suits may be evolved', Raymond Durgnat wrote in his *International Times* review of *Space – Place*, conjuring up the culture of Archigram and Warren Chalk's design for a self-contained living pod suit, the 'Suit-a-Loon', which was yet another variation on the techno-morphology of inflatables and the second skin.

For a while, in 1969, Mark Boyle had studio space at St Katherine's Dock. In November, he embarked on perhaps the most ambitious of all the visionary projects at the end of the decade. *Tidal Series* (1969) was the result of paradoxically fixing the surface of a sand bank at Camber Sands at different times during a given week. Using the infinite capacity of the sea's action to mould and rearrange the sand bank into unrepeatable patterns, Boyle and Joan Hills made two works a day, ultimately producing an elegiac series that paralleled Liliane Lijn's cosmic ordering. In the *Tidal Series*, the central topic of the thrust towards the 'dematerialisation of art' was realised; nature 'wrote' itself through indexical signs, impressions that were fixed by the same advances in plastics technology that had enabled the immaculate plastic sculptures of St Martin's. A chance choice of a fixed spot on the sand bank was, in its turn, endlessly randomised in the shifts of water, sand and organic life forms. Boyle saw the project as examining 'the effect of the elemental forces on the site'.[18] The result was a sublime, serial tracing of 'life', of these 'forces', of a literalising lyricism that restored a sense of cosmic pastoral beyond London.

Jeff Shaw and Graham Stevens,
Inflatable Structure, St Katherine's Docks, 1969

Jeff Shaw,
Inside a Pneumatic Structure,
1969

It was here, in this imaginary space of 'Pneumatics', that the Sixties 'free body' found its final apotheosis. Tumbling, disorientated, buoyed up against gravity, discovering a second, sculptural skin ...

Maurice Agis
and Peter Jones,
Spaceplace,
1967

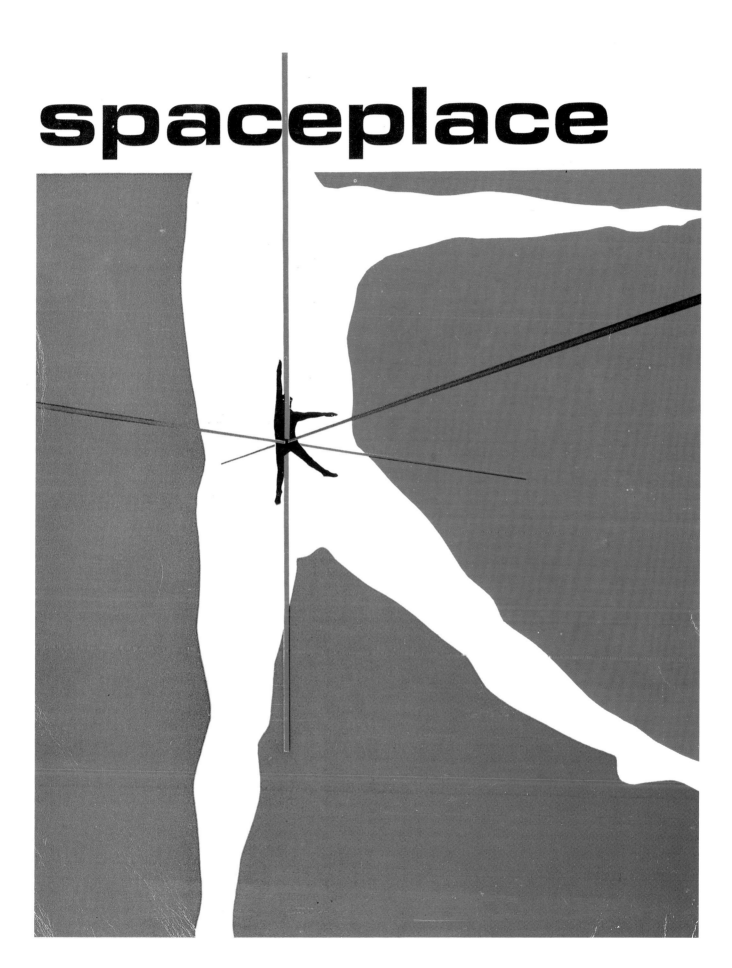

spaceplace

Maurice Agis and Peter Jones, **Space Place**, 1967

Maurice Agis and Peter Jones,
Space Place,
c.1970

200

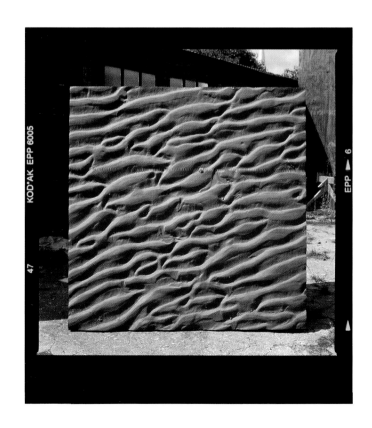

Mark Boyle and Joan Hills,
The Tidal Series, 1969–70
Sand and fibreglass, each 122 x 122 cm
Private collection

SPACE
Anthony Everitt, SPACE 1969

Even when there are no strikes, dockland usually appears deserted. The streets have that desolating emptiness which evokes the atmosphere of Sunday mornings, or the day after the Bomb. And nowhere more so than at St. Katherine's Docks by Tower Bridge in London. But for the last few months there have been indications that all is not as it should be. Hanging from a heavy iron gate, only too symbolic of the dead weight of commercial respectability, an irresponsibly yellow sign reads 'Buttercup Chain'. Young men in Jimi Hendrix hairstyles and tight velveteen jeans can be seen strolling down the cobbled street or issuing out of a grandly austere eighteenth-century warehouse which rises from the waters of the Thames like a utilitarian *palazzo*. Lewis Carroll and Franz Kafka would both have felt at ease if they had ever wandered inside, up the barrack-like staircase and down dark low stretches of seemingly endless space. At every turn, there is a surprise. Here, along a grimy corridor, is a mocked-up café which looks as if it is a stage set, constructed from *objets trouvés*, for an institutional Mad Hatter's Tea Party. Disappearing into the distance, a middle-aged American dream in lime green picks her elegant way with a matching parasol. In a cavernous and otherwise vacant gloom, a young man sits contemplating a bland canvas of colossal dimensions. If *this* is life in the docks, then it is no wonder that our exports are doing badly.

The mystery is easily explained. It is all a question of SPACE. That is (for the uninitiate), Space Provision (Artistic, Cultural and Educational) Ltd. This is an organisation which does exactly as its title announces and provides studio space for artist in the 60,000 sq.ft. available at the warehouse or at five other smaller offshoots. Peter Sedgley, the painter, found the building in May 1968 while looking for a studio of his own. But he immediately realised the possibilities and persuaded a formidable list of directors (including Bridget Riley, the artist, and Irene Worth, the actress) to help him negotiate a lease from the G.L.C The studios opened to artists in April 1969.

Of course there are problems. Everybody may have to move out in 18 months if the Council want the site back for re-development, and there is a shortage of money. The revenue from rent (5/- per sq.ft. per annum), from various Trusts and from the Arts Council have probably not been enough to prevent private cash from being spent. Nevertheless, the project has been enormously successful to date and there is a waiting list of two hundred. SPACE has (in a manner of speaking) filled a gap.

For whatever has been said about the indispensable creative advantages of deprivation, the artist has long wanted to leave his garret. But the inadequacy of modern patronage has made it difficult for him to do so. Leaving the cramped conditions at Art College, the average student cannot afford adequate studio space at a time when he most needs it. It is not surprising if, married with children and holding down a teaching job as his sole source of income, he has to limit production severely – if not actually stop it. It was Peter Sedgley's idea, that if all else failed, the artist should start looking after himself and become his own patron. SPACE's motto could well be 'Patronage of the artist, by the artist for the artist'.

Working space is only one among many problems. The most serious of all is the fragmentation (at every level) of the artistic scene. Because of poor communication, it is very hard for artists, especially in the provinces, to find the necessary contacts – for experimental materials and processes (...)

This is where AIR comes in – or, more fully, the Artists' Information Registry. Another of Peter Sedgley's ideas, it works in close co-operation with SPACE. The Registry is composed of an Artists' Index, which is a library of information, biographical, visual and even 'audio', about artists, for the benefit of sponsors and exhibition organisers, and Information Registry which lists useful Technical Information, Art Organisations, Sponsors etc., for the benefit of artists. There is also *Catalyst*, a useful booklet of artists and the like who perform, lecture, show films and so forth. So runs the theory. Unfortunately, although it was founded before SPACE in

1967, AIR has not yet left the ground. It costs money and time to establish comprehensive lists of this order – and at the time of writing, none of them are operative, except *Catalyst*.

Still, something is being done. If SPACE and AIR became permanent features, the effects would be far reaching. Art is not really a communal affair in England and the impact of such complete and instant communication between artist could not fail to be revolutionary. It is unwise to make any long term predictions, except perhaps to note that tightly knit communities tend to become exclusive and to acquire a fixed 'style'. But this is a risk which the organisers are very well aware of – and their only policy is not to have a policy. The potential benefits, on the other hand, are huge.

The future rightly counts for little beside the current reality, that artist are being given, or rather are giving themselves, practical assistance. 'I have never seen my pictures from so far off' is one painter's delighted response. In possession of as much room as he needs, away from the telephone and the pressures of domestic life, from pressures of any sort, he can sit down, think and work uninterruptedly. What more could any artist ask?

Celebration for Institutional Consumption
Stuart Brisley, Brighton Festival 1970 (described by the artist in 1992)

My entry into performance was in 1966. I abandoned the idea of constructing discrete objects because I had stumbled upon an irresolvable problem which necessitated an exploration into dematerialisation as a possible solution.

(...)

I had come to the conclusion that I needed to re-engage with the human element, not in terms of representation, but in actuality. The engagement with the figure which had begun in the life room in 1949 then passing into the perception of the edges or surfaces of one's own body reached from within in 1958, (although I wouldn't have described it in that way at the time) and represented in terms of `matter' painting and which had been abandoned six or so years previously would now be energised by using one's own body as vehicle and image.

(...)

Celebration for Institutional Consumption.
Structure
This event was structured as the annual dinner of an imaginary institution. As the dinner progressed it became apparent that the director was in effect also an inmate. Or at least the position of the director (of the work and of the institution) was ambiguous. The director merged into the inmates whose containment was not the institution but the terms of the society in which the institution existed.

Each participant was contracted to fulfil a set of tasks.

Plan of work: (from the original notes)

Phase 1 begins 30 minutes before dinner.
A continuous sound from sine generator. Low light in space. #5 minutes before dining figure is placed in cage suspended above dining table. Seating for 14.
Zero. Figures walk into hall – make their way slowly and in silence to the table. They are roped together and led by a controller who is

dressed as they are. All participants are dressed identically.

Each figure has a rope attached. They take their allotted seats and tie themselves to the table.

Soup is served

Three figures attach throat microphones to their throats to catch eating sounds. During this course everyone is silent and controlled. No words to be spoken.

The sine generator sound is faded out, and amplified eating noises faded in.

(...)
End of course. silence.

There is absolute silence and immobility between each course. (There is a possibility that sine generator noise maybe used during these in-between course periods.)

Plates are removed.

Controller climbs into cage and cuts into large anonymous figure with a knife.

All participants at table below take no notice of figure above at any time during the dinner. controller returns to seat.

Second course - fish - is brought in by 2 or 3 inmates.

Second course begins.

Figure rises, takes microphone, makes short statement expressing gratitude to sponsors of the Institution etc.

Sits down. eating begins.

After 3 or 4 minutes figure gets up, and begins to dance.

Two other inmates get up and mimic dancer. Sine generator is switched on high frequency as the sound is gradually turned down in scale (volume). The dancer and two mimics gradually return to seats signifying end of course.

During this course conversation between the diners may have taken place. One figure may have spent time knitting, another may have spent time under the table, etc.

End of course. Silence and immobility.
Plates are removed.

Controller climbs into cage, cuts into anony-

mous figure - intestines begin to hang down. Controller climbs down.

Third course - chicken - is served.

Figure rises, introduces everyone present, maybe tells joke, recites poem, etc.

He sits down. Eating begins.

Gradually participants get up from table - begin to go through individual rituals: one person speaks in Greek, a figure sings, figure dances, a figure examines food. Figure holds monologue to no one in particular, another gives a nonsensical speech. Another moves out towards the audience and begins to speak poetically (could be 'speaking in tongues'), makes noises, etc. All this is quite controlled. It must not appear to be extreme, but rather the meanderings of people who do not appear to recognise the dining conventions they operate within, and who do not feel aggressive.

Sine generator at very high pitch gradually comes down, signifies return to table to finish the third course.

End of course. Absolute silence and immobility.

Plates are removed.

Controller climbs into cage, cuts into figure severely. Stomach drops onto the table. Participants do not move, or make any sign of recognition of what is happening above. Controller returns to seat.

Fourth course – icecream – meringue is served.

Figure stands and makes speech which puts what has been happening into context. Makes someone comment about law/ order/ chaos/evolution etc.,

(The speech crystallised the dual position of director/ inmate.)

This speech is the major formal event of the dinner.

Inmates remain silent and respectful although those who have developed individual ritualised quirks will retain them.

Figure returns to seat.

Eating begins.

There is a sense of suppression about the proceedings at this point.

Stuart Brisley,
Celebration for
Institutional Consumption,
1970

Conversation takes place – people may move a little but not to the same extent as in the previous course.

End of course. Silence and immobility.

Controller climbs into cage.
Figure is divested of remaining clothing and is revealed as a nude female.
Controller returns to seat.
Coffee is brought in.
At this stage it is as though the participants have suddenly become aware of the audience.
They move out towards them and have the freedom to do what they will, provided that they maintain a separation between themselves and the audience.
This should be the course where all pretence to a voluntary involvement with the dining conventions is broken and chaos (hopefully) ensues.

At the relevant point the controller will use the sine generator high frequency sound to draw the participants back to the table where they untie themselves from the table are roped together and taken away.

3 participants return to bring down the figure in the cage.
The lights are dimmed.

The end of the dinner is when the participants leave the place.

Space Place
Maurice Agis and Peter Jones,
Museum of Modern Art, Oxford,
December 1966

This constructed space is our attempt to demonstrate an idea – the idea is a place for people – a place where you can meet – to look – to feel – to listen – to laugh – to cry – to love – to protest – a place for people.

The development of this idea is to construct places outside the imposed limits of art galleries and existing buildings. These places would allow full physical use of the structure which unfortunately the mechanics of this structure will not allow. We are developing a spatial language based on human proportion and size, which when used to construct active space relates a person to that space by extending from the smallest detail to the overall concept. This spatial language is a living language which develops through use. Space is made active by the tensioned relationships of the forms that articulate it asymmetrically, creating a sense of movement. By moving you effect the space and it effects you, developing your understanding of the nature of real space. An active space demands participation, it directs us to complete the incomplete by providing us with continuous changing spatial relationships. The asymmetrical order also implies relationships beyond those physically stated, suggesting the infinite extension of space. Asymmetrical order is a recognition of life as a process of growth, change, relatedness, not static, not finalized, not perfectible. An active spatial area can liberate our senses.

Space Place
Raymond Burgnat,
From a review in *International Times*,
December 1966

(...) The Space Place is created from horizontal and vertical rods and planes of colour, with taped music. As the spectator walks, sits, thinks, in it, the forms and sounds gently ease his perceptions which are unconsciously brace against the muddle, fuss and chaos of our everyday environment. It imposes nothing on him, no clutching hands.

For, perhaps, the first time in his life, he encounters an orderliness which is not prohibitive. The Place offers him forms which he can arrange. He enters as a passive spectator, becomes a freeman.

This freedom is a healthy alternative to current assumptions that the only freedom is in libidinal revolt.

Man from the 21st Century
Stephen Willats, 1969

(...)
The main objective of the project is to attempt to show two groups of people that are socially and economically and physically separated that they both share the same predicament which is that they are not in full control of their social environment. In other words, instead of exercising control over their social environment and determining their own behavioral strategies within it, their social environment is controlling their behaviour. It is hoped to build a meta-language between the two groups that allows an understanding of both of their social problems

The two areas selected are Hyson Green, which is a typical Victorian terraced working class area, and a new middle class housing development at Bramcote towards the outskirts of Nottingham. Other goals that the project has either thrown up or have been purposefully designed in to it are also seen as important for educational and propaganda reason. One of the most important of those is to show that the artist can effectively operate outside the confines of an (exclusive) art environment and can socially orientate a stance in terms of a societal context which is outside the traditional precedents which dictate a framework for operation.

In order that background information can be built up on the coding and habits of the two social groups, two questionnaires are being used: one dealing with leisure and shopping habits in order to see if the two groups already come into contact so that these areas can be used to build the meta-language. The other one is to try and determine restricted behaviours and codes, and is made up of face, clothes, shape and colour charts; people being asked to associate either a shape with a word or word to a shape.

The background information when sufficiently built up will then be given to a group of specialists to see what strategies and advice they can offer, given the object of the project. These consist of a cybertition, George Mallen (theoretical strategies); operational research, Stewart Pound (actual strategies); Julian

Miller, neurologist (behavioral psychology): Peter Whittle, perceptual psychologist (perceptual advice and strategies) and an advertising man (campaign organisation).

It is not known what actual strategies will be devised but groups will work within an overall strategy developing the proposals put forward by the specialist advisers.

It is intended to work within hue goal structure patterns and routines of behaviour that already exist in the two groups in order to cut back orientation and redundance. It is with this in mind that the canvassing of hue code questionnaire was conceived as a campaign called Man from the 21st Century, the canvassers dressing up in silver jump suits with helmets, and arriving in a street in a time machine.

It is felt that this way a better response can be achieved with the questionnaire than presenting the occupant with an artist. This was born out with the first questionnaire when the canvasser that dressed so as to typify an ideal and responsible middle class person did considerably better than the others who presented themselves as students.

(...)

Avant-Garde Casualties
The Times, Leader article,
30 September 1967

The recent closure of a number of galleries in London which have hitherto brought the work of the advance-guard of painters and sculptors to public notice should not pass without some comment. The exhibitions at these galleries have often had favourable mention. What they have shown is of the kind that in several instances has gained added respect for Britain abroad, as reflecting a lively condition of the arts and proving that a vigorous contemporary outlook prevails.

Why, it may be asked have the avant-garde galleries not fared better? The bleak answer seems inevitable that the work they have specialized in does not sell or sell in such quantity or at such a price as makes it a practical economic proposition. The reasons for this invite further inquiry. A possible conclusion is that the public is not interested. A somewhat different explanation may be found, however.

It is likely that a number of people view new conceptions of form and colour, experiments in optical effect and so on, with considerable interest but without the wish to acquire them personally. The numerous exhibitions of modern art have perhaps fostered the impression that it is a free communal entertainment. It is left to the modern museums to acquire examples of the new departures of the day, though they can absorb only a limited number.

Experiment, if that is the work for entirely free expression and unconventional handling of materials, is not a commodity like a Venetian view answering to a demand. It is always easy to put the blame for a lack of response on the Philistine. On the other hand, it may be argued that the self-centred attitude of the avant-garde artist who disclaims any wish to 'communicate' does not help to narrow the gap between him and the public. The phrase now in vogue, 'audience participation', seems to apply to the curiosity that works of an unusual nature arouse. What more it means is less certain.

There is always the possibility, too, that the sensations they go in for are merely ephemeral. Yet adventure in art needs its outlet. Painting and sculpture have as much right to the experimental attitude as science. There is not so much exhibition space accorded to the young artist with new ideas that one can view the disappearance of any of their partisans among the galleries without regret.

Chapter 1 Action

1 Anne Martin, interview with the author, 25 November 1991.

2 Robyn Denny/Dick Smith, 'An Open Letter to John Minton', **Newsheet**, December 1956, p 4.

3 Tim Scott, interview with the author, 27 July 1992.

4 Robyn Denny, interview with the author, 29 May 1992.

5 D. S. 'There are Vegetables at the Bottom of my Garden', **Newsheet**, December 1956, p 2.

6 Cf. 'Living City', **Living Arts** No. 2, Summer 1963, pp.76-7

7 Richard Smith, 'Paintings and Drawings by John Plumb', New Vision Centre Gallery, October 1957.

8 **Them** refers to the title of the science fiction horror film. Roger Coleman, 'Two Painters', **ARK** No. 20, Autumn 1957, p 26.

9 Lawrence Alloway, 'Personal Statement', **ARK** No. 19, Summer 1957, p 28.

10 Denys Sutton, Preface, **Metavisual Tachiste and Abstract Art**, Redfern Gallery, 1957, unpaginated.

11 Ibid.

12 Georges Mathieu, 'La Condamnation de Sigor de Brabant', **ARK** No. 20, Autumn 1957, pp 5-7, p 6.

13 Roger Coleman, interview with the author, 15 August 1992.

14 'Si ça coule ça coule', **Liberation,** 1er Aout 1958.

15 'Peinture à la flamme', **La Croix**, 31 Juillet 1958.

16 Roddy Maude-Roxby, 'Editorial', **ARK** No. 24.

17 Gustav Metzger, interview with the author, 12 November 1991.

18 'Flynn in Bitumen', **Daily Herald**, 8 December 1959.

19 Lawrence Alloway, 'Notes on Abstract Art and Mass Media', **Arts Review**, 27 February 1960.

20 Michael Chalk, op cit.

21 Stuart Brisley, **Text on Action Paintings and Performance Pieces**, July 1992, p 1.

22 Ibid.

23 Gwyther Irwin, 'Statement', '**3 Collagists**', ICA, November 1958.

24 Gwyther Irwin, interview with the author, 10 September 1991.

25 Lawrence Alloway, 'Situation in Retrospect', **Architectural Design**, February 1961, pp 82-3, p 82.

26 Roger Coleman, 'Two painters', op. cit., p 26.

27 Lawrence Alloway, 'New Trends in British Art', The New York-Rome Foundation, 1958, unpaginated.

28 Lawrence Alloway, 'Real Places', **Architectural Design**, June 1958, p 249.

29 Gillian Ayres, interview with the author, 20 July 1992.

30 Lawrence Alloway, 'Introduction' Gillian Ayres, Molton Gallery, October 1960.

31 For example of *écriture feminine*, Cf. the writings of Hélène Cixious, and Catherine Clément, **The Newly Born Woman**, 1987.

32 Gillian Ayres, 'Statement', **Situation**, Arts Council of Great Britain, 1962.

33 Ibid.

34 Lawrence Alloway, ibid.

35 Gillian Ayres quoted in Alloway, ibid.

Chapter 2   Dissent

1 Michael Middleton, **Eduardo Paolozzi**, 1962, unpaginated.

2 Gilles Deleuze, 'Active and Reactive', ed. D.B. Allison, **The New Nietzsche**, 1985, p 101.

3 Pat Arrowsmith, 'Auto-Destructive Art', **Peace News**, 22 July 1960.

4 Gustav Metzger, **Auto Destructive Art**, 4 November 1958.

5 Gustav Metzger, **Auto Destructive Art/A Talk at the London Architectural Association**, 1965, p 16.

6 Bertrand Russell, **Has Man a Future ?**, 1961, p 127.

7 E.g. Metzger's, '3 Paintings' at 14 Monmouth St, WC2, August 1959.

8 Recalled by Ken Garland, interview with the author, 6 May 1992.

9 Shown at New Vision Centre Gallery, January 1960, with gold-leaf paintings by Peter Blake.

10 John Russell, 'The Polemical Painter', *The Sunday Times*, 10 February 1963.

11 Ibid.

12 R.B.Kitaj, 'Two paintings with Notes', **Gazette**, No. 2, 1961, p 3.

13 Ibid.

Pauline Boty

Pauline Boty was born in 1938 and studied at Wimbledon School of Art and the Royal College of Art, London. She featured with Derek Boshier, Peter Blake and Peter Phillips in the BBC film *Pop Goes the Easel* in 1962 and in the BBC television programme *Monitor* in 1963.

Pauline Boty's first one-person show was at the Grabowski Gallery, London, in 1963. Selected group exhibitions include 'New Art 62', Festival of Labour, Congress House, London (1962), 'New Approaches to the Figure', Arthur Jeffress Gallery, London (1962), and 'Pop Art', Midland Group Gallery, Nottingham (1963).

Pauline Boty died in London in 1966.

Mark Boyle

Born in Glasgow in 1934, Mark Boyle spent three years in the Army before studying law at Glasgow University from 1955–56.

Mark Boyle's first one-person show was at the Woodstock Gallery, London, in 1963. Subsequent solo exhibitions and events include 'Suddenly Last Supper' (event), South Kensington, London (1964), Indica Gallery, London (1966), 'Dig' (event), Shepherd's Bush, London (1966), 'Bodily Fluids and Functions' (event), Roundhouse, London (1966) and the ICA, London (1970).

Mark Boyle is currently living and working in London.

Stuart Brisley

Stuart Brisley was born in Surrey in 1933 and studied at the Royal College of Art, London, the Akademie der Bildenden Kunst, Munich and Florida State University. He was a founder member of the Arts Information Registry (AIR) in 1967 and of the Artists Union in 1972 and a member of the Artist Placement Group (APG) from 1967–1971. Stuart Brisley's first solo exhibition was held at Studio F, Ulm, in 1961. Selected group exhibitions include 'K4', Brighton Festival (1967), 'Whsht' events, London (1966–69), 'Five Light Artists', Greenwich Gallery, London (1969), 'Celebration for Institutional Consumption', Brighton Palace Pier (1970) and 'Celebration for Due Process', London (1970).

Stuart Brisley is currently living and working in London.

Robert Brownjohn

Robert Brownjohn was born in Newark, New Jersey, in 1925. He studied at the Institute of Design, Chicago, and moved to London in 1961. After a brief spell working as Art Director at the J. Walter Thompson advertising agency, he moved to the McCann-Erickson agency. Whilst there he was commissioned on a freelance basis to do the titles for the James Bond film *From Russia with Love*, 1963. In 1964 he joined Cammell Hudson, a film production company, and soon after became a partner. Whilst there he produced titles for the next Bond film, *Goldfinger*. In the late 1960s he left to set up his own film/production office with David Nagata.

Robert Brownjohn died in London in 1970.

Sir Anthony Caro

Born in London in 1924, Anthony Caro studied sculpture at Regent Street Polytechnic and the Royal Academy School of Art, London. In 1951, whilst still at college, he became Henry Moore's assistant in London. In 1953 Caro began teaching sculpture part-time at St. Martin's School of Art, London (until 1956). He then taught at Bennington College, Vermont, USA, from 1963–64 (and spring 1965), and in 1968 resumed regular teaching at St. Martin's School of Art, London.

Caro's first solo exhibition was held in 1956 at the Galleria del Naviglio, Milan. Subsequent one-person exhibitions include Whitechapel Art Gallery, London (1963), André Emmerich Gallery, New York (1965, 1968), Washington Gallery of Modern Art (1965) and Kasmin Ltd., London (1967). Selected group exhibitions include 'New London Situation', Marlborough New London Gallery, London (1961), Venice Biennale, British Pavilion (1966), 'Primary Structures', Jewish Museum, New York (1966) and 'Noland, Caro and Morris Louis', Metropolitan Museum of Art, New York (1968).

Sir Anthony Caro is currently living and working in London.

Cora Wood,
Photograph of Anthony Caro,
1966

Patrick Caulfield

Patrick Caulfield was born in London in 1936 and studied at Chelsea School of Art, London, and the Royal College of Art, London. After graduating he travelled in Greece and Italy and then began teaching at Chelsea School of Art, London.

Patrick Caulfield's first one-person exhibition was held at the Robert Fraser Gallery, London, in 1965. Subsequent solo shows include Robert Fraser Gallery (1967) and Waddington Galleries, London (1969). Group exhibitions include 'Young Contemporaries', touring exhibition (1961, 1962, 1963) and 'The New Generation', Whitechapel Art Gallery, London (1964).

Patrick Caulfield is currently living and working in London.

Bernard Cohen

Bernard Cohen was born in London in 1933. He studied at St. Martin's School of Art, and the Slade School of Art, London. In 1955 he was awarded the University of London Boise Scholarship for one year's travel in Europe and in 1957 he returned to London after spending a few months in Rome. He taught part-time at Hammersmith School of Art, London, until 1960, and then at Ealing School of Art, London, from 1961–64, where he helped to design the Ground Course. He taught intermittently as a guest teacher at St. Martin's School of Art, London, in 1963, at Chelsea School of Art, London, 1966–1967 and began teaching at the Slade School of Art, London, in 1967. At the end of the 1960s, Cohen travelled across America, Canada and Mexico.

Bernard Cohen's first one-person exhibition was held at the Midland Group Gallery, Nottingham, in 1958. Subsequent solo exhibitions include Gimpel Fils, London (1958, 1960), Molton Gallery, London (1962), Kasmin Ltd., London (1963, 1964, 1967) and Betty Parson's Gallery, New York (1967). Selected group exhibitions include 'Dimensions', O'Hana Gallery, London (1957), 'Abstract Impressionism', University of Nottingham and Arts Council Gallery, London (1958), 'Situation', RBA Galleries, London (1960), 'New London Situation', New London Gallery, London (1961) and the XXXIII Biennale, Venice (1966).

Bernard Cohen is currently living and working in London.

Harold Cohen

Harold Cohen was born in London in 1928 and studied at the Slade School, London. After graduating in 1952 he began to teach and paint in London and Nottingham. In 1959 he was awarded a Harkness Fellowship by the Commonwealth Fund and went to live in New York until 1961 when he returned to Britain and began to teach at St. Martin's School of Art, London, the Slade School of Art, London, Ealing School of Art, and Bromley School of Art.

Harold Cohen's first one-person exhibition was held at the Ashmolean Musuem, Oxford, in 1950. Subsequent solo shows include Gimpel Fils Gallery, London (1954, 1956, 1958), Robert Fraser Gallery, London (1962, 1963, 1968), Whitechapel Art Gallery, London (retrospective) (1965) and Museum of Modern Art, Oxford (1968). Selected group shows include 'Dimensions', O'Hana Gallery, London (1957), 'Situation', RBA Gallery, London (1960), 'New London Situation', New London Gallery, London (1961) and the XXXIII Biennale, Venice, (1966).

Harold Cohen is currently living and working in California.

Michael Cooper

Michael Cooper was born in Huddersfield in 1941 and studied at Maidstone College of Art, Kent. During the early 1960s he taught at Maidstone College of Art, setting up their photographic department whilst there. In 1966 he was involved in photographic collaborations with Jim Dine at Robert Fraser Gallery, London, and in the same year began working as Fraser's gallery photographer. He photographed the Beatles' *Sergeant Pepper* album cover and *Their Satanic Majesties' Request* cover for The Rolling Stones in 1967.

Michael Cooper died in London in 1973.

John Cowan

John Cowan was born in Gillingham in 1929. After serving in the RAF, he worked in the 'rag' trade and civil engineering, and became a photographer in the late 1950s. During the 1960s, he worked for numerous commercial clients and publications including *Queen*, *Vogue*, *The Sunday Times* and *The Daily Express*, establishing a reputation for dramatic, energetic, black and white fashion images and portraits. His London studio was used by Antonioni as the principal location for the film *Blow-Up* (1966). He moved briefly to New York in late 1969 where he was taken up by Diana Vreeland for exotic location shoots for American *Vogue*.

One-person exhibitions include 'The Interpretation of Impact through Energy', Gordon Cameras, London (1960) and 'Exhibition of Photographs', Cookham (1970). He had a group show with Roger Mayne, Don McCullin and Raymond Moore at modfot one, London (1967).

John Cowan died in East Hagbourne in 1979.

Bill Culbert

Bill Culbert was born in New Zealand in 1935. He trained at the Royal College of Art, London.

Culbert's first one-person exhibition was held at the Commonwealth Art Gallery, London, in 1961. Subsequent solo exhibitions include Piccadilly Gallery, London (1963) and McRoberts and Tunnard Gallery, London, in 1965. Group exhibitions include 'Young Contemporaries', London (1959, 1960), 'K4', Brighton Festival, (1967) and 'Survey 68', Camden Arts Centre (1968). The last two exhibitions were in collaboration with Stuart Brisley.

Bill Culbert is currently living and working in France.

Robyn Denny

Robyn Denny was born in Surrey in 1930. He studied at St. Martin's School of Art and the Royal College of Art, London. He taught at Hammersmith College of Art 1957 - 59, at Bath Academy of Art 1959–65 and began teaching at the Slade School of Art, London in 1965. In 1966 he became a member of Art Panel, Arts Council of Great Britain.

Robyn Denny's first one-person exhibition was held at Gallery One, London, in 1957. Subsequent one-person exhibitions include Gimpel Fils, London (1958), Molton Gallery, London (1961), Kasmin Ltd., London (1964, 1969) and Robert Elkon, New York (1966, 1967). Selected group shows include 'Metavisual, Tachiste, Abstract', Redfern Gallery (1957), 'Dimensions', O'Hana Gallery (1957), 'Six From Now', Cambridge, 'Situation', RBA Galleries (1960), 'Art of Assemblage', Museum of Modern Art, New York (1961), 'New London Situation', New London Gallery, London (1961), 'Neue Malerei in England', Stadtisches Museum, Leverküsen (1961) and '7 junge englische Maler', Kunsthalle, Basle (1963), 'London: The New Scene', Walker Art Center, Minneapolis, USA and subsequent American tour (1965), 'Caro, Cohen, Denny, Smith', Kasmin Ltd., London, 'Four Englishmen', Galeria dell'Ariete, Milan (1966) and the British Pavilion, XXXIII Biennale, Venice (1966).

Robyn Denny is currently living and working in London.

Michael English

Michael English was born in Oxfordshire in 1941 and studied at Ealing College of Art, London. In 1967 he became involved in the hippy movement in England and the USA, illustrating psychedelic posters and painting fashionable shopfronts. He collaborated with Nigel Weymouth on *Osiris* posters in early 1967 and on *Hapshash and the Coloured Coat* later in the same year. In 1969, he produced a series of prints entitled *Food Synaesthetics* and *Rubbish*.

English's first one-person exhibition was held at the Motif Gallery, London,in 1969.

Michael English is currently living and working in London.

Alan Fletcher

Alan Fletcher was born in Nairobi, Kenya in 1931. He studied at the Royal College of Art, London and the School of Architecture and Design, Yale University. Fletcher began his career in New York where he worked for the Container Corporation, *Fortune Magazine* and IBM. Moving to London in 1959, he co-founded Fletcher/ Forbes/Gill, which served such clients as Pirelli, Cunard, Olivetti and Reuters. He is a founder member of Pentagram, formed in 1972.

Alan Fletcher is currently living and working in London.

Robert Freeman

Robert Freeman was born in London in 1936 and studied English Literature at Cambridge University. In 1960 he worked briefly as Programme Director at the ICA, London, before beginning his career in professional photography. His main assignments were with *The Sunday Times Colour Magazine*. In 1961 he made two short films, *Trailer* (with Richard Smith) and *Saga*. Freeman met the Beatles during their first English tour. It was photographs of John Coltrane and other jazz musicians that led to his three year association with them, designing and photographing five of their album covers and the title sequences for their two films – *A Hard Day's Night* and *Help!*

During this period he continued with other photographic commissions, including work for *Nova* magazine and *The Sunday Times Colour Magazine*.

Robert Freeman designed the title sequence for Richard Lester's *The Knack*, which won the Palme D'Or at the Cannes Film Festival in 1965, and filmed the title sequence for *The Night of the Generals*. From 1967–69 he directed three feature films for 20th Century Fox; *The Untouchables*, scripted by Ian La Frenais (1967), *The World of Fashion* produced by Darryl Zanuck (1968), and *Secret World* starring Jacqueline Bisset and scripted by Gerard Brach (1969).

Robert Freeman is currently living and working in Spain.

Ken Garland

Born in Southampton in 1929, Ken Garland studied at Central School of Art, London after three years of military service (1947–50). He was Art Editor for the National Trade Press, London 1954–56 and Art Editor of *Design* magazine 1956–62. From 1962 he was in practice as the design consultancy, Ken Garland and Associates, whose clients included Galt Toys (1962–82), the Ministry of Technology (1962–67) and Borough of St. Pancras/London Borough of Camden (1964–67).

Ken Garland is currently living and working in London.

William Green

William Green was born in 1934 and studied at Sidcup School of Art and the Royal College of Art, London, with a year working in an architect's office in between. From 1959 to 1962 Green taught at Harrow and Ealing Schools of Art.

William Green's first one-person exhibition was held in 1958 at the New Vision Centre Gallery, London. Subsequent solo exhibitions include 'The Errol Flynn Exhibition', New Vision Centre Gallery, London (1959). Selected group exhibitions include 'Exhibition of Contemporary British Art', Rome–New York Art Foundation, Rome (1957), 'Dimensions', O'Hana Gallery, London (1957), 'Situation', RBA Galleries, London, (1960) and 'Situation', Arts Council touring exhibition (1962–63). Television work includes the Ken Russell film *Painting an Action Painting* and a Pathe Pictorial newsreel (1957).

William Green is currently living and working in London.

Richard Hamilton

Richard Hamilton was born in London in 1922. He studied in London at Westminster Technical College, St. Martin's School of Art, the Royal Academy School of Art and the Slade School of Art, London. In 1952 he began teaching at Central School of Art, and a year later at King's College, University of Durham, Newcastle upon Tyne (until 1966). From 1957 to 1966 he also taught at the Royal College of Art, London. Hamilton made his first visit to the USA in 1963.

Richard Hamilton's first one-person exhibition was 'Variations' on the theme of the grim reaper at Gimpel Fils, London, in 1950. Subsequent solo exhibitions include Hanover Gallery, London (1955, 1964), University of Durham, Newcastle upon Tyne (1955), Robert Fraser Gallery, London (1966, 1969), Studio Marconi, Milan (1969) and Tate Gallery, London (1970). Selected group exhibitions include 'An Exhibit', Hatton Gallery, Newcastle upon Tyne (1957) and 'Exhibit 2', Hatton Gallery, Newcastle upon Tyne (1959).

Richard Hamilton is currently living and working in Oxfordshire.

Raymond Hawkey

Raymond Hawkey was born in Plymouth in 1930 and studied at the Royal College of Art, London. He was Art Editor for *Vogue* 1954–57, Art Director for Coleman, Prentis and Varley 1958–1959, Design Director for *The Daily Express* 1959–64 and Presentation Director for *The Observer* and *The Observer Colour Magazine* 1964–75.

Raymond Hawkey is currently living and working in London.

Peter Hobbs

Peter Hobbs was born in London in 1930 and after working as a jazz pianist from 1953 to 1955, studied at Central School of Art, London. He taught at Central School of Art (1960–61) and Camberwell School of Art, London (1963–66).

Hobb's first one-person exhibition was held at ICA, London, in 1960. Subsequent solo exhibitions include Molton Gallery, London (1961) and selected group exhibitions include 'Situation', Arts Council touring exhibition (1962–63).

Peter Hobbs is currently living and working in London.

David Hockney

David Hockney was born in Bradford in 1937. He studied at Bradford College of Art and the Royal College of Art, London. In 1961 he made his first visit to New York, and in 1963 travelled to Egypt to produce drawings for *The Sunday Times*. He left England to live in Los Angeles in 1963. The following year he taught briefly in Iowa, and in 1965, at Colorado University. He returned to live in London in 1968.

Hockney's first one-person exhibition was held at Kasmin Ltd., London, in 1963. Subseqent solo exhibitions include Alan Gallery, New York (1964) and Kasmin Ltd., London (1965). Selected group shows include 'Young Contemporaries', London (1960–62), 'Image in Progress', Grabowski Gallery, London (1962), Third Paris Biennale des Jeunes (1963), 'The New Generation', Whitechapel Art Gallery, London (1964) and 'London: The New Scene', Walker Art Center, Minneapolis and subsequent American tour (1965–66).

David Hockney is currently living and working in Los Angeles.

Sir Howard Hodgkin

Howard Hodgkin was born in London in 1932. He studied at Camberwell School of Art, London and Bath Academy of Art. He taught at Charterhouse School, Surrey, 1954–56, at Bath Academy of Art 1956–66 and at Chelsea School of Art, London 1966–72.

Howard Hodgkin's first one-person exhibition was held at Arthur Tooth and Sons, London, in 1962. Subsequent one-person shows include Arthur Tooth and Sons (1964, 1967) and Kasmin Ltd., London (1969). Selected group exhibitions include 'Critic's Choice', Stone Gallery, Newcastle (1963) and 'London: The New Scene', Walker Art Center, Minneapolis and subsequent American tour (1965–66).

Sir Howard Hodgkin is currently living and working in London.

Richard Hollis

Richard Hollis was born in London in 1934. He studied at Wimbledon and Central School of Art, London, and became involved in graphic design whilst running his own silk-screen press. He taught lithography at the London School of Printing 1958–61, worked as a freelance designer in London from 1958 and in Paris from 1963–64. In 1964 he was made Head of Graphic Design at West of England College of Art, Bristol and 1966–68 was Art Editor of *New Society*. He returned to London to teach graphic design at Central School of Art, London (1968–78) and to freelance.

Richard Hollis is currently living and working in London.

Gordon House

Gordon House was born in South Wales in 1932. He studied at Luton School of Art, Bedfordshire and St. Albans School of Art, Hertfordshire. From 1951-1952 he worked as a sculptor's assistant and from 1959 was Graphic Designer for Kynoch Press, Birmingham. He was a part-time tutor at Central School of Art, London, Hornsey School of Art, London, and Luton College of Technology, Bedfordshire, 1961–63. He also worked as a painter, printmaker, and design consultant in London during the 1960s. House's first one-person exhibition was held at New Vision Centre Gallery, London, in 1959. Selected group exhibitions include 'Situation', RBA Galleries, London (1960), 'Neue Malerie in England', Stadtisches Museum, Leverküsen (1961), 'New London Situation', Marlborough New London Galleries, London, 'Four London Artists', Marlborough-Gerson Gallery, New York (1968) and 'Play Orbit', ICA, London (1969).

Gordon House is currently living and working in London.

John Hoyland

John Hoyland was born in Sheffield in 1934 and studied at Sheffield College of Art, the Royal Academy Schools, London, and at evening classes at Central School of Art, London. In 1960 he began teaching basic design at Hornsey College of Art, London, and at Oxford School of Art, and in 1962 started teaching at Croydon School of Art and at Chelsea School of Art, London (where he was made Principal Lecturer in 1965). Hoyland visited the USA for the first time with a Peter Stuyvesant Bursary in 1964, and made his first works in New York in 1967.

John Hoyland had his first solo exhibition in 1964 at the Marlborough New London Gallery, London. Selected group exhibitions include 'Situation', RBA Galleries, London (1960), 'Neue Malerei in England', Leverküsen (1961), Marlborough New London Gallery, London (1962), 7th Tokyo Biennale (1963) and 'The New Generation', Whitechapel Art Gallery, London (1964).

John Hoyland is currently living and working in London.

228

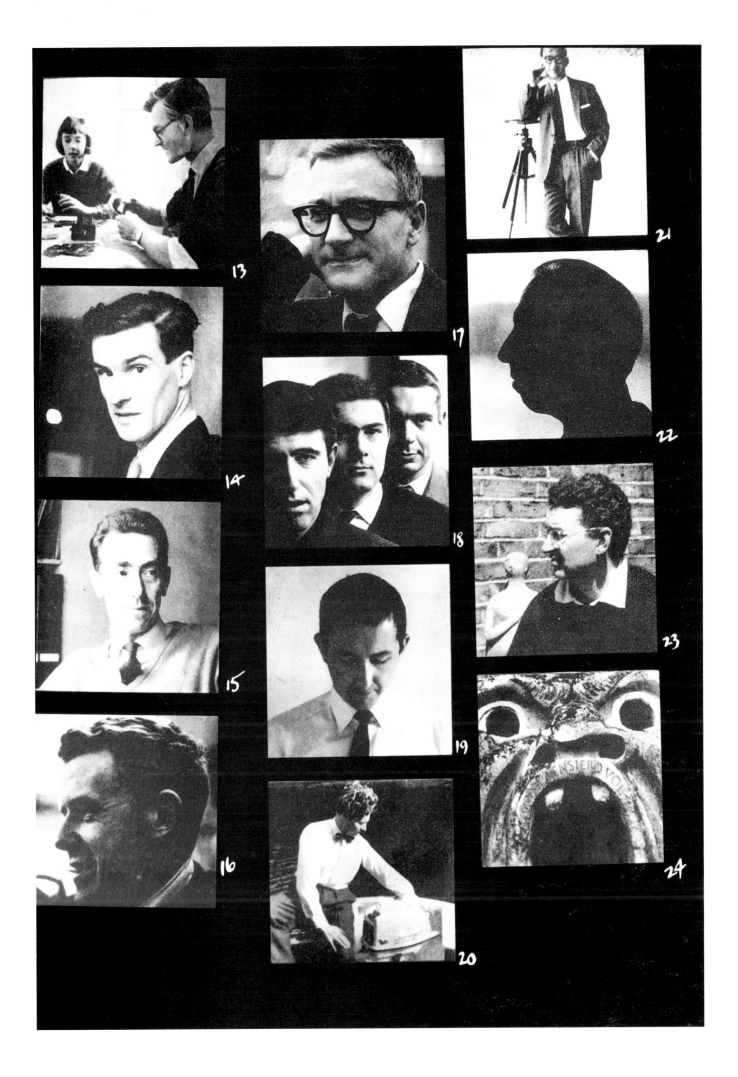

Gwyther Irwin

Gwyther Irwin was born in Basingstoke in 1931 and studied at Central School of Art, London. He taught intermittently at Bath Academy of Art and at Chelsea and Hornsey Schools of Art, London, 1951–54. Irwin began making collages in 1957 and from 1965 to 1968 designed and cut *Rectangular Relief* in Portland Stone for British Petroleum House, London. Irwin was made Head of Fine Art at Brighton Polytechnic, East Sussex, in 1969.

Gwyther Irwin's first one-person exhibition was at Gallery One, London, in 1957. Subsequent one-person exhibitions include Gimpel Fils, London (1959, 1962, 1963) and the XXXII Venice Biennale, British Pavillion and European tour (1964). Selected group shows include 'Metavisual, Tachiste, Abstract', Redfern Gallery, London (1957), 'Dimensions', O'Hana Gallery, London (1957), 'Three Collagists', ICA, London (1958), 'Situation', RBA Galleries, London (1960) and 'The Art of Assemblage', Museum of Modern Art, New York (1961).

Gwyther Irwin is currently living and working in London and Cornwall.

Tess Jaray

Born in Vienna in 1937, Tess Jaray studied at St. Martin's School of Art and the Slade School of Art, London. After graduating in 1960, she travelled in Italy with an Abbey Minor Travelling Scholarship. The following year she was awarded the French Government Scholarship and worked in William Hayter's *atelier* in Paris. Jaray began teaching at Hornsey College of Art in 1962.

Tess Jaray's first one-person exhibition was at Grabowski Gallery, London, in 1963. Subsequent solo shows include Hamilton Galleries (1965, 1967) and selected group exhibitions include 'Neue Malerei in England', Leverküsen (1961), Grabowski Gallery, London (1963) and the Ninth Tokyo Biennale (1967).

Tess Jaray is currently living and working in London.

Allen Jones

Allen Jones was born in Southampton in 1937 and studied at Hornsey School of Art and the Royal College of Art, London. After teaching at Croydon College of Art (1961–63) and Chelsea School of Art, London (1964), Jones went to live in the USA. During 1968–70 he was a visiting teacher at Hochschule fur Bildende Kunst, Hamburg, and a Guest Professor at the Department of Painting, University of South Florida. In 1970 Jones designed the set and costumes for the play *O Calcutta!* in London, and designed the German television production *Männer wir kommen* in WDR, Cologne.

Allen Jones's first solo exhibition was in 1963 at Arthur Tooth and Sons, London. Subsequent one-person exhibitions include Arthur Tooth and Sons (1964, 1967) and Richard Feigen Gallery, Chicago (1965). Selected group shows include 'Young Contemporaries', London (1960, 1961), 'Two Young Figurative Painters', ICA, London (1962), 'Image in Progress', Grabowski Gallery, London (1962), 'The New Generation', Whitechapel Art Gallery, London (1964), 'London: The New Art Scene', Walker Art Center, Minneapolis and subsequent American tour (1965–66) and 'Structure 66', The Welsh Arts Council, Cardiff (1966).

Allen Jones is currently living and working in London.

Michael Kidner

Michael Kidner was born in 1917 in Northamptonshire. He studied History and Anthropology at Cambridge and Landscape Architecture at Ohio State University, USA. After serving in the Canadian Army 1941–1946, he studied briefly at Goldsmith's College, London. He lived in Paris between 1953–55, attending André Lhote's *atelier* intermittently for six months. He became influenced by the exhibitions at the Tate Gallery, London, of American Abstract Expressionism in 1957 and 1959. Kidner began teaching part-time at Leicester Polytechnic in 1963 and at Bath Academy of Art in 1964. He began to make his first interference patterns, stripe and wave paintings in 1963 and co-founded the Systems Group with Jeffrey Steele and others in 1969.

Michael Kidner's first one-person exhibition was held at St. Hilda's College, Oxford, in 1959. Subsequent solo shows include Grabowski Gallery, London (1964) and Axiom Gallery, London (1967). Selected group shows include Grabowski Gallery, London (1962), 'The Responsive Eye', Museum of Modern Art, New York (1965) and 'Kinetic Art', Herbert Art Gallery, Coventry (1966).

Michael Kidner is currently living and working in London.

Phillip King

Phillip King was born in Tunis in 1934. After two years of National Service he returned to study Modern Languages at Cambridge University, and to study at St. Martin's School of Art, London. He began working as an assistant to Henry Moore in 1958 and in 1960 was awarded a Boise Travelling Scholarship which he used to travel to Greece. He began teaching at St. Martin's School of Art, London, in 1959, taught a term at Bennington College, Vermont, in 1964 and was awarded the Peter Stuyvesant Foundation Bursary in 1965. He was made a Trustee of the Tate Gallery, London, in 1967 (until 1969) and began teaching at the Slade School of Art, London, in the same year.

Phillip King's first one-person exhibition was held at Heffer's Gallery, Cambridge, in 1957. Subsequent solo shows include Rowan Gallery, London (1964), Richard Feigen Gallery (1966) and the British Pavillion, XXXIV Venice Biennale (1968). Selected group shows include 'The New Generation', Whitechapel Art Gallery, London (1965), 'London: The New Scene', Walker Art Center, Minneapolis (1965–66) and 'Primary Structures', Jewish Museum, New York (1966).

Phillip King is currently living and working in London.

R.B. Kitaj

R.B. Kitaj was born in Ohio, USA in 1932. He studied at the Cooper Union Institute, New York, the Academy of Fine Arts, Vienna, and later at the Ruskin School of Drawing, Oxford, and the Royal College of Art, London. He taught at Ealing School of Art, Camberwell School of Art, and the Slade School of Art, London, 1961–67. He left London to work at the University of California for a year in 1967, and was visiting Professor there in 1970.

Kitaj's first exhibition was held at the Marlborough New Gallery, London, in 1963. Subsequent solo exhibitions include Marlborough-Gerson Gallery, New York (1965), Los Angeles County Museum, (1965), Stedelijk Museum, Amsterdam (1967) and the University of California, (1967). Selected group exhibitions include 'Young Contemporaries', London (1960–61).

R.B. Kitaj is currently living and working in London.

Bruce Lacey

Bruce Lacey was born in London in 1927. He studied at Hornsey School of Art and the Royal College of Art, London. He began making short comedy films for television and appearing as a comic cabaret performer from 1956. In 1964 he appeared in the opening programme of BBC2 with the comic jazz musicians, The Alberts, and made the first version of his robot for the International Poets Convention at the Albert Hall. In 1968 he was awarded an Arts Council grant to make *Journey through the organs of the human body* for the City of London Festival and in 1970 demonstrated his robots at the International Broadcasting Convention, London, with his wife Jill Bruce on the radio mike as the voice of the robot. The ICA held an evening of his films in the same year.

Bruce Lacey's first one-person exhibition of assemblages was held at Gallery One, London, in 1964. Subsequent exhibitions include Marlborough New London Gallery, London (1966), 'Swinging London', Madame Tussauds, London (1968) and 'Then Sitting Rooms', ICA, London (1970). Selected events and happenings include the 'Coffin Event' for Irish night at the Satire Club, on the streets of London, (1959), the 'Paper Event' with Tinguely, ICA, London (1959), 'Operation' with Keith and Heather Musgrove, Jill Bruce and John Latham (organised by Jeff Nutthall), Better Books, Charing Cross Road, London (1964) and Robot Events as part of 'Whsht' evenings (organised by Peter Kuttner, 1967–68).

Bruce Lacey is currently living and working in Norfolk.

Gerald Laing

Gerald Laing was born in Newcastle upon Tyne in 1936. After serving in the army, he studied at St. Martin's School of Art, London. He went to live in New York in 1964 and was artist in residence at Aspen Institute for Humanistic Studies in 1966. He returned to Britain to live in Scotland in 1969.

Laing's first one-person exhibition was at Laing Municipal Art Gallery, Newcastle, in 1963. Subsequent solo shows include ICA, London (1964) and Richard Feigen Gallery, New York (1964, 1965, 1967, 1969) and Richard Feigen Gallery, Chicago (1966, 1970). Selected group exhibitions include 'Young Contemporaries', London (1963) and 'Primary Structures', Jewish Museum, New York (1966).

Gerald Laing is currently living and working in Scotland.

John Latham

John Latham was born in 1921 in Africa. After serving in the Royal Navy (1940–46) he studied in London at Regent Street Polytechnic and Chelsea College of Art, London. He visited New York and Washington for the first time in 1961, and in 1964 performed his first burning of book sculptures. In 1967 he co-founded the Artist Placement Group (APG) and began teaching at St. Martin's School of Art, London, in the same year.

John Latham's first one-person exhibition was held at the Kingsly Gallery, London in 1951. Subsequent solo exhibitions include Kasmin Ltd., London (1963) and group shows include 'The Art of Assemblage', Museum of Modern Art, New York (1961–62). Selected events and happenings include 'First Skoob Tower Ceremonies', Oxford, Edinburgh and London (1964), 'Skoob Tower Ceremonies' and the performance 'Film' during the Destruction in Art Symposium, London (1966), 'Still and Chew', chewing of Clement Greenberg's book *Art and Culture* with friends and students from St. Martin's School of Art, London (1966-67), Actions at Better Books, Charing Cross Road, London (1967) and *APG's* 'Industrial Negative Symposium' at the Mermaid Theatre, London (1968).

John Latham is currently living and working in London.

Roger Law

Roger Law was born in Cambridgeshire in 1941 and studied at Cambridge School of Art. During the 1960s, Law worked on *The Observer* as a cartoonist before moving to *The Sunday Times Colour Magazine* in 1965. One-person exhibitions include making '... a huge exhibition of myself in various Soho public houses'. He was involved in forming the Luck and Flaw partnership which later led to the development of the *Spitting Image* television satire show.

Roger Law is currently living and working in London.

Liliane Lijn

Liliane Lijn was born in New York in 1939. She studied Archaeology and Art History at the Sorbonne and the Ecole du Louvre, Paris, and taught herself to draw. In 1961–62 she went to live in New York and produced her first work with light, reflection and motion. She began working in Paris in 1963, moved to Athens in 1964 and then settled in London in 1966.

Lijn's first one-person exhibition was held at La Librarie Anglaise, Paris, in 1963. Subsequent solo exhibitions include Indica Gallery, London (1967) and Hanover Gallery, London (1970). Selected group exhibitions include 'Light and Movement', Museum of Modern Art, Paris (1967) and 'Kinetic Art', Hayward Gallery, London (1970).

Liliane Lijn is currently living and working in London.

Anne Martin

Anne Martin was born in London in 1936. She studied at the Royal College of Art, London, and on graduating in 1959 was awarded the Abbey Minor Scholarship to travel to Rome. The following year she was awarded the French Government Scholarship and conducted research into the Surrealist roots of Abstract Expressionism (including a discussion with André Breton). She began teaching at Central School of Art, London, in 1966.

Anne Martin's first one-person exhibition (selected by William Green) was held at the Royal College of Art library, London in 1957. Selected group exhibitions include 'Young Contemporaries', London (1958, 1959) and 'Some Moore Rejects', Open Studio Vernon Yard, London (1963).

Anne Martin is currently living and working in London.

Roddy Maude-Roxby

Roddy Maude-Roxby was born in London in 1930. He studied at the Royal College of Art, London, and was President of the Royal College Theatre Group whilst there. He became Editor of *ARK* magazine in 1958. From 1967 he taught at CURE, Paddington Day Centre, London.

Maude-Roxby's first two-person exhibition was with Peter Blake at the Portal Gallery, London, in 1960. Selected theatre productions during the 1960s include *One Way Pendulum*, and *One Leg Over the Wrong Wall*, Royal Court, London (1960), *The Establishment*, Greek Street, London (1963), *The Knack*, New York (1964), *Miniatures*, Royal Court, London (1965), *Help Stamp Out Marriage*, Booth Theatre, New York (1966) and *The Three Sisters*, Royal Court, London (1967).

Roddy Maude-Roxby is currently living and working in London.

Anne Martin,
State of Place, 1960
Oil on canvas,
183 x 183 cm,
Private collection

Linda McCartney

Linda McCartney was born in New York in 1941. She studied Fine Art at Arizona University, developing an interest in photography whilst there. During the 1960s, McCartney worked in Manhattan as a freelance photographer for magazines such as *Rolling Stone*, and was resident photograper at Fillmore East, Manhattan.

Linda McCartney is currently living and working in Sussex.

Don McCullin

Donald McCullin was born in 1935 and studied at Hammersmith School of Art, London. He was a photographic assistant in aerial reconnaissance with the RAF 1953–55, and turned freelance, working for *The Observer*, in 1961. In 1964, he joined *The Sunday Times* as a contract photographer, and became particularly well known for his in-depth coverage of wars and other 'hard news' subjects. He has photographed in the Congo, Vietnam, Cambodia, Biafra, India, Pakistan, Northern Ireland, and other 'trouble spots'.

Donald McCullin is currently living and working in Dorset.

Tony Messenger

Tony Messenger was born in London in 1936 and studied at the London College of Printing and the Royal College of Art, London. During the 1960s, Messenger worked as a designer for *Ambassador* magazine and produced illustrations for the BBC.

Messenger's first one-person exhibition was held at the Trafford Gallery, London, in 1957. Selected group shows include 'Young Contemporaries', London (1955, 1956, 1957, 1958).

Tony Messenger is currently living and working in London.

Gustav Metzger

Born in Nuremberg, Germany in 1926, Gustav Metzger emigrated to Britain in 1939. He studied at Sir John Cass Institute, London, Borough Polytechnic, London, Anglo-French Art Centre, London, Antwerp Academy, and at Oxford School of Art. A painter until 1957, he became dissatisfied with the results and began to practise and theorise about auto-destructive works. He acted as Secretary to the Destruction in Art symposium, London, in 1966 and was Editor of *PAGE*, the bulletin of the Computer Arts Society, London, 1969–72

Metzger's first one-person exhibition was held at 14 Monmouth Street, London, in 1959. Subsequent solo shows include Temple Gallery, London (1960), 'Auto-destructive art', Better Books, London (window display) (1965) and 'Liquid Crystals in Art', Lamda Theatre Club, London (1966). Group exhibitions include 'Event 1: Computer Arts Society', Royal College of Art, London (1969).

Gustav Metzger's current whereabouts are unknown.

Lewis Morley

Born in Hong Kong in 1925, Lewis Morley left the RAF to study Graphic Design at Twickenham College. After graduating in 1952 he worked as a commercial artist in an advertising agency. He became a regular contributor to *Tatler* from 1958, worked as a fashion photographer for *Go!* (edited by John Anstey) in 1961 and worked regularly for *She* magazine from 1962.

Lewis Morley is currently living and working in Australia.

Eduardo Paolozzi

Eduardo Paolozzi was born in Edinburgh in 1924. He studied at Edinburgh College of Art and at the Slade School of Art, London, and moved to Paris in 1947. He returned to London in 1949 to begin teaching textile design at Central School of Art, London, leaving in 1955 to teach sculpture at St. Martin's School of Art, London. He was Visiting Professor at the Hochschule fur Bildende Künste, Hamburg, 1960–62, and Visiting Lecturer at the University of California in 1968.

Paolozzi's one-person show was at the Mayor Gallery, London, in 1947. Subsequent solo exhibitions include Robert Fraser Gallery, London (1964), Hanover Gallery, London (1967) and Alecto Gallery, London (1967).

Eduardo Paolozzi is currently living and working in London.

Peter Phillips

Peter Phillips was born in Birmingham in 1939. He studied at Birmingham College of Art and the Royal College of Art, London. After graduating in 1962 he began teaching at Coventry College of Art and Birmingham College of Art. He went to live in New York in 1964 after being awarded a Harkness Fellowship and travelled in North America with Allen Jones in 1965. He moved to Zurich in 1966 after forming Hybrid Enterprises with Gerald Laing (1965–66) and 1968–69 was a Guest Professor at Hochschule fur Bildende Künst, Hamburg.

Peter Phillips' first one-person exhibition was held at the Kornblee Gallery, New York, in 1965. Subsequent solo exhibitions include the Kornblee Gallery, New York (1966) and Galerie Bischofberger, Zurich (1968, 1969). Selected group shows include 'Young Contemporaries', London (1962) and 'Today and Yesterday', Arthur Tooth and Sons, London (1962).

Peter Phillips is currently living and working in Zurich.

Roland Piché

Roland Piché was born in London in 1938. He studied at Hornsey College of Art, and the Royal College of Art, London, with a year working in Montreal with the sculptor, Gaudia, in between. He was a part-time assistant to Henry Moore 1962–63 and began teaching at Maidstone School of Art, Kent, in 1964.

Piché's first one-person exhibition was held at Marlborough New London Gallery, London, in 1967. Selected group exhibitions include 'Young Contemporaries', London (1963, 1964), 'New Generation', Whitechapel Art Gallery, London (1966, 1968) and 'Summer Exhibition', Marlborough-Gerson Gallery, London (1965).

Roland Piché's current whereabouts are unknown.

John Plumb

John Plumb was born in Bedfordshire in 1927. He studied at Byam Shaw School of Drawing and Painting, and Central School of Art, London. Part-time teaching posts included Central School of Art, London (1955–58 and 1966–68), Luton School of Art (1955–61) and Maidstone College of Art, Kent (1961–66). He took up a post as Visiting Professor at Bennington College, Vermont, in 1968 and on returning to England in 1969 was made Senior Lecturer in Painting at Central School of Art, London.

John Plumb's first solo exibition was held at the New Vision Centre Gallery, London, in 1957. Subsequent one-person shows include Gallery One, London (1957), New Vision Centre Gallery, London (1959), Molton Gallery, London (1961), Marlborough New London Gallery, London (1964) and Axiom Gallery, London (1966, 1968). Selected group shows include 'Situation', RBA Galleries, London (1960), 'New London Situation', Marlborough New London Gallery, London (1961), *Mural for the International Union of Architects Congress*, South Bank, London (1961), 'New Painting in England', Leverküsen Museum, West Germany (1961), 'Hoyland, Plumb, Stroud, Turnbull', Marlborough New London Gallery, London (1962) and 'New Forms of Shape and Colour', Stedelijk Museum, Amsterdam (1966–67).

John Plumb is currently living and working in Shepperton.

Bridget Riley

Born in London in 1931, Bridget Riley studied at Goldsmith's School of Art, and the Royal College of Art, London. She worked intermittently at an advertising agency 1959–64 and in 1963 was awarded the AICA Critics' prize. The following year she was awarded the Peter Stuyvesant Foundation Travel Bursary to the USA and in 1968, the International Prize for Painting at the XXXIV Biennale, Venice.

Bridget Riley's first one-person show was held at Gallery One, London, in 1962. Subsequent solo exhibitions include Richard Feigen Gallery, New York (1965, 1967), Robert Fraser Gallery, London (1966), British Pavillion, XXXIV Venice Biennale (1968) and Rowan Gallery, London (1969). Selected group shows include 'The New Generation', Whitechapel Art Gallery, London (1964), 'The Responsive Eye', Museum of Modern Art, New York (1965) and 'London: The New Scene', Walker Art Center, Minneapolis and subsequent American tour (1965–66).

Bridget Riley is currently living and working in London.

Ralph Rumney

Ralph Rumney was born in 1934 in Halifax and studied at the Halifax School of Art. At the beginning of the 1950s he registered as a Conscientious Objector and lived between France, Italy and London (partly to avoid being arrested for avoiding conscription). He was a founder-member of *Internationale Situationniste* in 1957, and in

1959 became involved in 'Place' in collaboration with Robyn Denny and RichardSmith, Lawrence Alloway and Roger Coleman. From 1969 he worked for French broadcasting producing programmes for the English language service.

Ralph Rumney's first one-person show was held at Galleria Apollinaire in 1956. Group shows include 'Metavisual, Tachiste, Abstract' at Redfern Gallery, London (1957).

Ralph Rumney is currently living and working in the South of France.

Gerald Scarfe

Gerald Scarfe was born in London in 1936 and studied at the Royal College of Art, London. He made drawings for *Punch* magazine and *Private Eye* in the late 1950s and early 1960s and joined *The Daily Mail* as a political cartoonist in 1966. He made on-the-spot drawings in Vietnam and in 1967 joined *The Sunday Times* as a political cartoonist making reportage drawings in Northern Ireland and covering the Six Day War in the Middle East and the cholera epidemic in Calcutta. In 1968 he worked for *Time* magazine, New York. He designed the costumes for the play *Ubu Unchained* at the Traverse Theatre in 1967 and in 1968 co-wrote and animated *I think I see Violence All Around Me* for the BBC.

Scarfe's first one-person exhibition was held at Horse Shoe Wharf Club, London (1966). Subsequent solo exhibitions include Grosvenor Gallery, London (1969) and Motif Editions Gallery, London (1970). Selected group shows include 'Violence in Contemporary Art', ICA, London (1964) and 'Heroes Live', Madame Tussauds, London (1967).

Gerald Scarfe is currently living and working in London.

Tim Scott

Tim Scott was born in London in 1937. He studied architecture at the Architectural Association and sculpture under Anthony Caro at St. Martin's School of Art, London. He moved to Paris after graduating in 1959 and on his return in 1961 began teaching part-time at St. Martin's School of Art, London. He was awarded the Peter Stuyvesant Foundation Bursary in 1965.

Tim Scott's first one-person exhibition was held at Waddington Galleries, London, in 1966. Subsequent solo exhibitions include Whitechapel Art Gallery, London (1967) and selected group shows include '26 Young Sculptors', ICA, London (1961), 'Mixed Exhibition', Molton Gallery, London (1964), 'The New Generation: 1965', Whitechapel Art Gallery (1965) and 'Primary Structures', Jewish Museum, New York (1966).

Tim Scott is currently living and working in London.

Peter Sedgley

Peter Sedgley was born in London in 1930 and studied building and architecture at Brixton School of Building. He worked as an architectural assistant in the 1950s and from 1960–62 initiated a small Co-operative of Associated Technicians concerned with design and constuction. A self taught painter, he concentrated on painting from 1963. In 1968 he was a founder member of SPACE, a charitable organisation for provision of studio and work space in the arts, and of AIR, an information centre of the arts in general and documentation of practising artists.

Peter Sedgley's first one-person exhibition was held at McRoberts and Tunnard Gallery, London, in 1965–66. Subsequent solo shows include Redfern Gallery, London (1968) and selected group shows include 'Seven 64', McRoberts and Tunnard Gallery, London (1964), 'The Responsive Eye', Museum of Modern Art, New York (1965), 'Opening Show', Axiom Gallery (1966), 'Ten 66', McRoberts and Tunnard Gallery, London (1966), 'Kinetic Art', Herbert Art Gallery, Coventry (1966), 'Redfern Summer Show', Redfern Gallery, London (1968) and 'Five Light Artists', Greenwich Gallery, London (1969).

Peter Sedgley is currently living and working in Berlin.

Colin Self

Colin Self was born in Norwich in 1941. He studied at Norwich School of Art and the Slade School of Art, London, and from 1962–1965 travelled widely in Canada and the USA. He was awarded prizes for drawing at the Paris Biennale in 1968 and for etchings at the International Print Biennale, Bradford, in 1969.

Self's first solo exhibition was held at the Piccadilly Gallery, London in 1966. Subsequent solo shows include those at the Robert Fraser Gallery, London (1967) and Galerie Yvon Lambert, Paris (1967). Group exhibitions include 'Summer Show', Kasmin Ltd. (1964), Robert Fraser Gallery, London (1965) and 'New Idioms', Robert Fraser Gallery, London (1966).

Colin Self is currently living and working in Norfolk.

Tony Bisley,
Photograph of Richard Smith
painting at the RCA, 1956–57

Sylvia Sleigh

Sylvia Sleigh was born in 1916 in Llandudno, North Wales and studied at Brighton School of Art, East Sussex.

Sleigh's first one-person exhibition was at Trafford Gallery, London, in 1962. Subsequent solo exhibitions were held at Crystal Palace Gardens, London (1962), Bennington College, Vermont (1963), Bryon Gallery, New York (1965) and Hemmingway Gallery, New York (1968, 1969, 1971). Selected group exhibitions include 'American Landscapes', Bryon Gallery, New York (1965), 'The Box Show', Bryon Gallery, New York (1966) and 'Portraits from the American Art World', The New School of Social Research Art Center, New York (1966).

Sylvia Sleigh is currently living and working in New York.

Richard Smith

Richard Smith was born in Hertfordshire in 1931. He studied at Luton School of Art, St. Albans School of Art and the Royal College of Art, London. On graduating in 1957 he was awarded the Royal College of Art Scholarship for travel in Italy. He taught mural decoration at Hammersmith College of Art, London, 1957–1958 and in 1959 was awarded the Harkness Fellowship of the Commonwealth Fund for travel in the USA. On his return to London in 1961 Smith spent two years teaching at St. Martin's School of Art, London. He returned to the USA in 1963 and from 1967-68 taught at the University of Virginia and the University of California, after which he moved back to England. Smith was awarded the CBE in 1971.

Richard Smith's first one-person exhibition was held at Green Gallery, New York in 1961. Subsequent solo shows include Artist's studio, Bath Street, London (1962), ICA, London (1962), Kasmin Ltd., London (1963, 1967, 1969), Green Gallery, New York (1963, 1965), Whitechapel Art Gallery, London (retrospective) (1966) and Richard Feigen Gallery, New York (1966, 1968). Selected group shows include 'Dimensions', O'Hana Gallery, London (1957), 'New Trends in British Art', New York Foundation, Rome (1957), 'Abstract Impressionism', Arts Council Gallery, Carlisle (1958), 'Place: A Collaboration', ICA, London (1959), 'Situation', RBA Galleries, London (1960), 'New London Situation', Marlborough New London Gallery, London (1961), 'Caro, Cohen, Denny, Smith', Kasmin Gallery, London (1966) and XXXIII Biennale, Venice (1966).

Richard Smith is currently living and working in New York and Aspen, Colorado, USA.

Herbert Spencer

Herbert Spencer was born in London in 1924. He served in the RAF from 1942–45 and founded *Typographica* magazine in 1949. From 1949–55 he taught typography once a week at Central School of Art, London. During the 1960s, he was typographical advisor to the RIBA, to the Universities of East Anglia and Leeds and to the Corporation of London Barbican Committee. He represented Britain at the First International Conference on Typography, New York (1958) and was a speaker at the Vision Conference at Southern Illinois University (1965) and at the Vision Conference, New York (1967). Spencer was appointed Senior Research Fellow at the Royal College of Art, London, in 1966 and was Editor of *The Penrose Album* from 1964–73.

Spencer's first one-person exhibition was held at Zwemmer Gallery, London in 1953. Herbert Spencer is currently living and working London.

Ralph Steadman

Ralph Steadman was born in Cheshire in 1936. He studied at East Ham Technical College and London College of Printing, London. A freelance cartoonist and illustrator, he worked for *Punch* magazine, *Private Eye* and *The Daily Telegraph* during the 1960s. Steadman was artist in residence at the University of Sussex in 1967.

Selected books illustrated by Steadman during the 1960s include *Fly Away Peter*, Dobson (1964), *Nord Sud Verlag* (published as *The Big Squirrel and the Little Rhinoceros*), Norton (1965), Daisy Ashford's *Where Love Lies Deepest*, Hart Davis (1966), Lewis Carroll's *Alice in Wonderland*, Dobson (1967) and *The Tale of Driver Grope*, Dobson (1969). Selected books written and illustrated by Steadman include *Ralph Steadman's Jelly Book*, Dobson (1967), *Still Life with Rasberry*, RPP and Whiting (1969) and *The Yellow Flowers*, Dobson, (1968).

Ralph Steadman is currently living and working in Kent.

Joe Tilson

Joe Tilson was born in London in 1928. After three years service in the RAF he studied at St. Martin's School of Art and the Royal College of Art, London. He was awarded a scholarship to travel to Rome after graduating in 1955, after which he lived and worked in Italy and Spain, to return in 1958. From 1959–63 he taught at St. Martin's School of Art and in 1962–63 was a Guest Lecturer at the Slade School of Art, London, and at Kings College, University of Durham, Newcastle upon Tyne. He lectured at the School of Visual Arts, New York, in 1966 and from 1971–72 was a guest teacher at the Hochschule fur Bildende Künst in Hamburg. Tilson participated in the BBC film Monitor in 1963 and was a member of the Art Panel, Arts Council from 1966. Joe Tilson's first one-person exhibition was held at Marlborough Gallery, London in 1962. Subsequent solo shows include Marlborough New Gallery, London (1962, 1966, 1970) and XXXII Venice Biennale (1964). Selected group exhibitions include 'British Painting in the Sixties', Whitechapel Art Gallery, London (1963), 'London: The New Scene', Walker Art Center, Minneapolis and subsequent American tour (1965–6).
Joe Tilson is currently living and working in London.

William Tucker

William Tucker was born in Cairo in 1935. He studied History at Oxford University and sculpture at Central School of Art and St Martin's School of Art, London. In 1961 he worked at the Victoria and Albert Museum, and began teaching at Goldsmith's College of Art and St. Martin's School of Art, London, in 1962. He was awarded the Peter Stuyvesant Foundation Bursary in 1965 and appointed Gregory Fellow at Leeds University 1968–70.
William Tucker's first one-person exhibition was held at Grabowski Gallery, London, in 1962. Subsequent solo shows include Rowan Gallery, London (1963, 1966), Richard Feigen Gallery, New York (1965) and Kasmin Ltd., London (1967, 1970). Selected group shows include '26 Young Sculptors', ICA, London (1960–61), 'New Generation: 1965', Whitechapel Art Gallery, London (1965), 'Primary Structures', The Jewish Museum, New York (1966) and 'Documenta IV', Kassel, West Germany (1968).
He is currently living and working in Willow, USA.

William Turnbull

Born in Dundee, Scotland, in 1922, William Turnbull studied at the Slade School of Art, London. After graduating in 1948, Turnbull lived and worked in Paris, returning to London in 1950. From 1950–61 he taught experimental design as a visiting artist at the Central School of Art and Crafts, London, teaching sculpture at the same school from 1964–72. He became a member of the Independent Group in the 1950s, and made his first visit to the USA in 1957.
William Turnbull's first one-person exhibition was held at the Hanover Gallery, London, in 1950. Subsequent solo shows include Hanover Gallery, London (1952), ICA, London (1957), Molton Gallery, London (1960, 1961), Marlborough Gerson Gallery, London (1961), IX Bienal, San Paolo (1967), Waddington Galleries, London (1967, 1969, 1970) and Hayward Gallery, London (1968). Selected group exhibitions include 'New Trends in British Art', New York-Rome Art Foundation, Rome (1958), 'Situation', RBA Galleries, London (1960), 'Sculpture in the Open Air', Battersea Park, London (1960), 'New London Situation', Marlborough New London Gallery, London (1961), 'Neue Malerei in England', Stadtisches Museum, Leverkusen (1961), 'Hoyland, Plumb, Stroud, Turnbull', Marlborough New London Gallery, London (1962) and '4 Documenta', Kassel, West Germany (1968).
William Turnbull is currently living and working in London.

Mark Vaux

Mark Vaux was born in Swindon, Wiltshire, in 1932 and studied at the Slade School of Art, London. He was awarded the Boise Scholarship to travel to Italy in 1961 and from 1962–72 taught at Bath Academy of Art and Hornsey College of Art, London.
Vaux's first one-person exhibition was held at Grabowski Gallery, London, in 1963. Subsequent solo shows include Hamilton Galleries, London (1965) and Axiom Gallery, London (1967, 1970). Selected group shows include 'Situation', RBA Galleries, London (1960), 'Situation', Marlborough New London Gallery, London (1961) and 'Neue Malerei in England', Städtisches Museum, Leverküsen (1961).
Mark Vaux is currently living and working in London.

Nigel Waymouth

Nigel Waymouth was born in Kasauli, India, in 1941 and studied at University College, London. During the late 1960s he worked as an illustrator and decorator. Shop fronts designed by him include Granny Takes A Trip, London, Indica Bookshop, London, and Breezes Bookshop, Brighton. He undertook graphic work for IT and OZ magazines during the 1960s. In early 1967 he collaborated with Michael English on Osiris posters and as Hapshash and the Coloured Coat in late 1967.
Waymouth's first one-man show was held at Fischer Fine Art, London, in 1977.
Nigel Waymouth is currently living and working in London.

Stephen Willats

Stephen Willats was born in London in 1943 and studied at the Ground Course, Ealing School of Art, London. From 1965, Willats has been editor and publisher of Control magazine.
Willats' first one-person exhibition was held at the Chester Beatty Research Centre, London, in 1964. Subsequent solo shows include 'Visual Automatics and Visual Transmitters', Museum of Modern Art, Oxford (1968). Selected group exhibitions include 'Kunst Licht Kunst', Stedelijk Museum, Amsterdam (1966), 'K4', Brighton Festival (1967), 'Public Eye', Kunsthaus, Hamburg (1968), 'Five Light Artists', Greenwich Theatre Art Gallery, London (1969), 'British Movements', Onnasch Gallery, Berlin (1969) and 'Kinetic Art', Hayward Gallery, London (1970).
Stephen Willats is currently living and working in London.

95

=